Brush Up Your Ayrshire

The (more or less) definitive guide
to visitor attractions
and things to see and do
in Ayrshire, Arran, Bute and Cumbrae,
including Robert Burns attractions.

by
Andy Baird

Westward
Media Limited

ISBN 0-9540474-1-9

BRUSH UP YOUR AYRSHIRE
by Andy Baird

© Andy Baird 2002

Published by
Westward Media Limited,
3 Five Roads,
Kilwinning,
Ayrshire,
Scotland
KA13 7JX

ISBN Number 0-9540474-1-9

Photographs: Andy Baird and Nick Smalley
Layout and artwork: Westward Media Limited

The author gratefully acknowledges the assistance given by the representatives of attractions featured in this book and also the support of those businesses who have placed advertising within the publication.

Please note that although every possible effort has been made to ensure that the information contained in this book is complete and up to date at the time of printing, neither the author, the publishers or their representatives accept any responsibility or liability for any alterations to opening times or changes in any specification or detail in respect of any of the attractions featured herein.

Contents

To Pat,
for her patience, understanding and encouragement,
with love.

Also to Alan and Marie,
who unintentionally provided the
circumstances for the idea.

Brush
Up
Your
Ayrshire

Introduction

The American playwright Thornton Wilder once suggested that when you were safe at home you wished you were having an adventure, but when you were having an adventure you wished you were safe at home. The minute he'd said it, he realised that, all things being equal, most ordinary travellers would agree with the first part, but disagree with the second part. Ergo, it was maybe a silly thing to say. He was embarrassed, and never said it in company again, but by then the damage was done, and his ill-conceived statement had made it into several books of quotes, where it remains to this day. Now truthfully, this has nothing to do with Ayrshire, but hey, it got your attention didn't it?

You will have noticed the title of the book. It took a lot of thought, the rejection of many alternatives, and more than a glass or two of wine. It is cleverly named as such, so that if you are a resident of Ayrshire or just a casual visitor, you have the opportunity to increase your knowledge of this part of Scotland. The book is a guide to most things that are worth seeing and doing in Ayrshire, Arran, Bute and Cumbrae. My intention is to inform, entertain and even educate you a little, and maybe dispel a few myths along the way. Quite deliberately, I have not rated restaurants or bars, however worthy, for the simple reason that food and drink and 'atmosphere' are much more a matter of personal preference, so I'll leave it to others to put their heads above the parapet on that one. Nobody has paid me to write about them (unfortunately!), and nobody has tried to influence me one way or the other. Any opinions expressed are my own, but I'm sure you'll find broad agreement with them, as I'm a reasonable kinda guy.

I assume you will have a car and a decent map, maybe even vice versa. I like the Official Tourist Leisure Maps published by Estate Publications, and which are available in most bookshops, large newsagents, and well-stocked petrol stations. The best one for this area is number 17 in the series. It's called Burns Country, and covers Ayrshire and Dumfries & Galloway, but unfortunately, only part of Bute. There is a separate map for Arran. There are however, basic maps in this guide, and I have given brief details of public transport. Beware though - public transport outwith the main towns is at best, patchy, and taxis are expensive. I also assume that you are a family - what we call 'Maw, Paw and the Weans' - and maybe even Gran and Grandad too, so you should find interesting things suitable for all ages and all members of your party. I read somewhere that the Scottish tourist industry earns something in the region of two and a half billion pounds yearly (very useful when Independence comes), so thank you very much for the contribution which I hope you're about to make! Whichever part of the world you come from, a warm welcome to you, and I'm sure you'll have an enjoyable time. You will find Ayrshire people very friendly, generally.

The county of Ayrshire is the county of my birth and where I choose to live. Administratively, it is divided into North Ayrshire, East Ayrshire, and South Ayrshire. There is no West Ayrshire. That would be ridiculous - you'd be in the middle of the Firth of Clyde, and nobody lives there anyway. It is a roughly crescent-shaped area in south-west Scotland, roughly 63 miles long, and roughly 26 miles at its widest, (roughly 100 km by 40 km) with roughly 376,500 of a population. True, there are other scenically spectacular areas of Scotland, but you can't beat the view of Arran and the Clyde islands from the hills, and no other area has our particular combination of lumpy bits, flat bits, empty bits, and a wet bit down one side. (Sounds like my first wife!)

The Gulf Stream sea current has a sizeable coastal influence here. It means that, in the sheltered open, we can grow palm trees and other plants which might struggle a bit in other areas. Actually, that's not strictly true. By the time it gets from the Gulf of Mexico to here, it's called the North Atlantic Drift, and also, they're not palm trees, but New Zealand Cabbage trees. Anyway, our coastal winters do tend to be less severe than in some other parts of the UK. In turn, this affects the thickness of our underwear and what is worn around the knees during the sporran-dangling season, or at least, its TOG rating. It is also the reason why Prestwick International Airport, or Glasgow Prestwick as it's confusingly known, is almost never closed by bad weather.

Digressing for a moment, many people may not know that Prestwick Airport is hallowed ground. In 1960, a young American Army Sergeant stepped off a plane from Germany on his way home, having finished his National Service. The airport was also an American Air Force base in those days, and the Sergeant had a couple of hours to wait while the plane was refuelled. Nothing unusual in that, you might think, except that this young man was The King - Elvis Presley, and despite some claims that he never visited Britain, THAT was the one and only time he ever touched British soil. There's a plaque in the airport to commemorate the event, or if you want to see pictures, go to www.rockmine.music.co.uk/Elvi.html

Speaking of transport links, you may like to combine your visit to Ayrshire with a trip to Ireland. The Seacat ferry service to Belfast, from where there are good road links to Dublin and other cities, runs from Troon several times per day, and you will avoid the long trek down the coast to Stranraer, the other exit point. Contact any travel agent for details.

Apart from the larger attractions, and maybe a few buildings and places associated with Scotland's National Poet, Robert Burns, most of Ayrshire is mostly unknown to most people, which is mostly a shame, as it's a county rich mostly in historical heritage and importance. Up until the Industrial Revolution of the 19th Century, Ayrshire was a farming and rural county, and had many large estates owned by so-called noble, but certainly powerful and often ambitious - i.e. aggressive - families. With the development of large reserves of coal, though, Ayrshire became an important and busy industrial region. Those industries are now long gone of course, and even today, we have difficulty getting and keeping skilled jobs.

Ayrshire has many famous sons - we claim William Wallace, as does neighbouring Renfrewshire, but we have hard evidence to help prove the claim. For instance, it is a matter of historical fact that the Wallace family of that time had lands at Ellerslie near Kilmarnock, but Renfrewshire appears to have 'invented' their connection only in the 19th Century. I have also heard a theory that - hold on to your seats, folks - Wallace was the model for a largely-fictitious Robin Hood! If that was true, it would really upset quite a few people, not least the English, but I know no more than that. Ask the guides at Dean Castle - that's where I heard the story! There is also a theory that Old King Cole of the children's nursery rhyme was in fact King Coilus, a Briton who ruled in these parts around 700AD. With impunity though, we can confidently lay claim to King Robert the Bruce; John Loudoun Macadam, the inventor of 'tarmac' roads and potholes; Robert Burns, poet; John Boyd Dunlop, inventor of the pneumatic tyre and punctures (caused of course, by Macadam's potholes, but more of Dunlop later); Thomas Makdougall Brisbane, Governor of New South Wales; John Galt, novelist; Alexander Macmillan, founder of the famous publishing firm; David Dale, cotton magnate and industrial welfare reformer; William Murdoch, inventor of the first steam car and the developer of gas lighting; Johnnie Walker, Kilmarnock whisky blender and the man personally responsible for making Scotsmen think they love everyone on New Year's Eve; and Alexander Fleming, discoverer of mouldy bread, which he later named penicillin. There are many other Ayrshire men and women who have influenced the human world in some way, though perhaps they are less well known. To return to Dunlop, recently published information reveals that he didn't "invent" the pneumatic tyre at all. 43 years after Robert Thomson of Kincardineshire took out a patent on a kind of pneumatic tyre in 1845, Dunlop came up with a broadly similar idea. Unfortunately, Dunlop sold the idea soon after, and like Thompson, missed the opportunity to profit from it. So again, don't believe everything you read in encyclopaedias and reference books.

Ayrshire products are known world-wide too - Johnnie Walker whisky of course; Dunlop cheese, nothing to do with tyres though, and now known as Scottish cheddar; Ayrshire early potatoes (the Gulf Stream's influence again!); Ayrshire dairy cattle, now largely replaced by Friesian; and Mauchline curling tongs - sorry, curling stones, (see entry, 'Burns House, Mauchline'). We have some of the most famous championship golf courses in the world at Troon, Prestwick and Turnberry. We have The World's Oldest Railway Bridge Over A River, Laigh Milton bridge near Kilmarnock, built in 1808. Crossing the River Ayr south of Mauchline, we have another Railway Bridge Double Record Breaker. Built in 1847, Ballochmyle Bridge is Britain's highest at 169 feet (51.5m), and in its day, it had the world's longest masonry span at 181 feet (55m). We have some absolutely fantastic beaches of sand, pebbles, shells, rocks and sewage, sometimes all at once. I have to admit that, at the time of writing, very few beaches reach European Union regulations about cleanliness, but they're working on it! In reality though, a much larger risk of swimming in the Firth of Clyde is hypothermia, Gulf Stream or no Gulf Stream!

Gaelic hasn't been spoken in Ayrshire for many, many hundreds of years, and most words or names have long since been Anglicised. About the only place you'll see Gaelic place names is on Arran and Bute. The signs in the Co-op supermarket in Brodick on Arran are duplicated in Gaelic - bread, biscuits, sugar, paperware, etc - and the name of the Arran ferry is painted in Gaelic on the ship's side. The islands have a more recent Gaelic heritage - indeed, many of the hills and mountains have Gaelic names - and the signs are an attempt to keep the language alive. If you're tempted to go walking in any of our lovely hills, or even the ugly ones, you're welcome, but please be sensible, and always be prepared for the weather turning bad even in 'Summer'. Remember to follow the Country Code - guard against fire, keep dogs under control, close all gates and take your litter home with you, that sort of thing. Oh, and don't pick wild flowers - it's illegal.

If this is your first visit from overseas, there are several things you should know. The Scots are famous throughout the world for their hospitality and friendliness; indeed, during the 1998 Soccer World Cup, the Scotland fans were voted the Best Behaved by international journalists. If your knowledge of Scotland has only been gleaned from movies or TV, you'll find the reality totally different. (For instance,

William Wallace didn't live in the Highlands, his father didn't speak with a broad Northern Ireland accent, he didn't paint his face blue or walk around in a kilt, and he didn't fall in love with that French Princess, as she was only a child. Also, he was a foot and a half taller than Mel Gibson!) Whole books have been written about the Scots' contributions to every aspect of human society, for instance, eleven UK Prime Ministers. Even a partial list of Scottish inventions is long - television, the photocopier, radar, the telephone, the fax machine, filmed adverts, the steam engine, colour photography, the national Banks of England, Scotland and France, lawnmowers, the game of golf, antiseptic, hypodermic syringes, Insulin, and many, many other worthy things. It's also true that the building of North America and Australasia couldn't have happened without us. Twenty US Presidents had Scots blood, not to mention two signatories of the Declaration of Independence, John Paul Jones, the Father of the American Navy, and several Governors of Australian States. So be careful - if you walk around saying "Hoots mon, ock aye the noo Jock", or speaking like Scotty from Star Trek, at best you'll get a surly scowl, and at worst you'll discover that "Shut yer stupit mooth" doesn't mean "Gosh, that's really funny, please repeat it constantly". And another thing - nowhere in Scotland will you find Brigadoon. It's another patronising and insulting Hollywood cliché. While we're on the subject, please try to avoid buying those tartan hat and red wig combinations which you'll find in many gift shops. They're called Jimmy hats for reasons far too complicated to go into here, and they're extremely naff, and only Scotland football fans can get away with wearing them. In truth, there are too many tatty "souvenirs" on sale, so please choose carefully. OK, OK, I'll calm down. End of sermon.

If you go into pubs, don't initiate conversations with the locals about cricket, religion or politics, even though we've got our Parliament back (there's a lot wrong with it!). And stay off football. Talk about the weather, everyone's got an opinion on that, or midgies. If you don't know what midgies are, don't worry, you'll find out. (In North America, they're called no-see-ums, so that should give you a clue!) If you admit you're not sure what haggis is, you're likely to be spun a yarn about a small creature with wings and fur and one leg shorter than the other so's it can run along hillsides! It's a little-known fact that haggis was a favourite on the menu in Greece centuries ago, and was very popular in England before Burns popularised it, so it's not even a Scottish 'invention'. Truthfully, haggis isn't half as revolting as most people make out, not if you think about what goes into your average burger or sausage!

Now, a word of warning - if you're "furrin", an old Scots word meaning, "Welcome, kind stranger, please open your wallet"(!), I hope you've brought plenty money with you, or have taken advantage of another invaluable Scottish invention, the bank overdraft. A recent quality Sunday newspaper survey found that travel within the UK is the most expensive in the world. Apparently, rail fares are about double those in the U.S., and at least 60% more than in the rest of Europe, while travel by road can cost eight times as much as in the U.S., and at least 20% more than in Europe. In fact, fares on Britain's privately-owned railways are the highest in the world, most services are unreliable, and many people, like me, find UK rail travel a deeply unpleasant experience. But then, no pain no gain.

To be completely serious for a moment, two disasters in 2001 had severe side effects on the UK tourist industry. As was widely reported, Foot and Mouth Disease devastated British farming, virtually closing down the countryside, though it appears that Ayrshire wasn't as badly affected as some parts of the UK. But the outbreak caused many operators to complain that tourism was suffering far worse than farming, there being no compensation for loss of earnings, and many attractions, visitor centres and hotels reported cancellations or huge drops in attendance. Many also stated they were unsure if they could continue in operation in 2002 and beyond.

The September 11th terrorist atrocities in New York and Washington could still have some ongoing effect on tourist numbers also, as many attractions rely heavily on North American and other overseas visitors.

At the time of writing though, (March 2002), the whole UK has been declared free of Foot and Mouth, and travellers seem to be returning gradually to the skies. As far as I can ascertain, all the attractions in the book will be open for business in 2002, but I cannot be held responsible if some of them think otherwise. If you're planning a special journey, particularly to a privately-owned attraction, phone ahead first.

Finally - the information contained here is, to the best of my knowlege, correct and accurate. If you come across any glaring omissions or inaccuracies though, please accept my apologies. If you want to make a comment of some kind, drop me a line via my publishers, and I'll fix it for next time. If it's a fair, constructive comment or even a compliment, thank you. If not, your mother was a hamster and your father smelled of elderberries, OK?

How to use this book

This humble tome is intended as no more than a **guide**, a **taster**, to what you will see, and most places you visit will have more detailed information than is contained here. Each entry has a brief explanation, with a bit of background or history to place   it in context, and details of opening times, prices, and location.

Most places are well signposted by the widely-seen official Tourist Board signs of white letters on a brown background, and a thistle symbol. The smallest of these is about four feet long, the largest the size of a small Principality. Many attractions have a Tourist Board Approved, Commended or Highly Commended blue thistle plaque displayed prominently too, so that's an extra guarantee of quality. One or two places may not be signposted too well, but this doesn't mean they are not worth seeing.
ALL the places in the book are worth seeing, depending on your interests, obviously. If you get lost, nearby locals will be happy to tell you where to go - er, I mean, give you directions.

(Incidentally, don't be fooled by yellow signs with black lettering, apparently pointing the way to what looks like a large, posh house or country mansion. They look similar to official Automobile Association signs, but without the AA logo on them, so you'll merely find yourself directed to the latest fancy housing development.)

Every effort has been made to be as accurate as possible when it comes to prices or opening times or what's available, so it's pointless blaming me or my publishers if somebody's been and gone and changed it. Admission prices vary widely, and most places have concessions for children, OAP's, families, etc. If an attraction is free, I say so, (indeed, at the back of the book, there's an at-a-glance list of free attractions), otherwise the key to the pricing symbols is as follows:

£ - under £2.
££ - between £2 and £3.
£££ - between £3 and £5.
££££ - between £5 and £10.
£££££ - over £10.

Sorry I can't be more accurate than that, but places may change their prices from season to season or even in or out of the school holidays.

You will find that, generally speaking, dogs are not allowed at visitor attractions, except perhaps in parks or gardens, and even then, there may be restrictions. The only exceptions to this rule will be guide dogs, so if this applies to your party, I strongly advise you to check before your visit. Most places have ample free parking and toilets, and it should be obvious which will have neither. Generally, most staffed premises keep office hours, which means approximately 9 to 5. Country Parks and the like usually stay open longer in Summer. On the plus side though, you will seldom come across The Three Least Desirable Words In The Universe - Closed For Lunch (unlike The Five Greatest Words In The Universe - Your Cash Has Been Counted). We seem to have largely abandoned that practice, except in the 'off' season, of course. Fortunately, restaurants and many pubs serve food all day, but you should beware of the frustrating, "The-kitchen-closed-thirty-seconds-ago-so-hard-luck-pal" experience.

Entries are listed in a roughly north to south direction. This is not to say that I expect you to be travelling this way, but it means that, unlike guides with alphabetised entries, all the attractions in the same general area will be found on adjacent pages. This way, it should be easy for you to get the most out of a particular area. There are separate sections on Burns, Arran, Bute and Cumbrae.

At the back of the book is an appendix of useful addresses, websites, and many other bits of information. Elsewhere, you should find discount vouchers for some attractions.

1
The Prophet's Grave
Near Largs

This is the grave of the 28-year-old Reverend William Smith, a church minister in Largs when plague, possibly Typhus, decimated the population in 1644. He refused to leave the dying while those who were unaffected fled in fear, but he caught the disease himself of course, and was the last person to die a few years later.

Hang on a minute though - if everybody else was dead or had moved away, how do we know he was the <u>last</u> to die? ..... oh, I'm confused .....

Anyhow, the fears and concerns caused by the epidemic of those days are quite well documented. In neighbouring parishes, old Town Council minutes have recorded cases of people being fined heavily for straying into the Largs area without official permission. Typhus came to Europe around 1490, via soldiers who had been fighting in Mediterranean countries. It was spread by lice, fleas, or mites, things that we all had in plenty in those days, and thrived in poor areas where conditions were particularly unsanitary. Its symptoms include severe headache, high fever, delirium, vomiting, and vicious knee trembling.

So far, it sounds remarkably similar to a very bad hangover, but typhus is contagious, and most spectacularly, involves the eruption of large red rashes on the skin (and believe me, I've toned <u>that</u> down a bit!). It was also called prison fever or ship fever, due to the exceedingly unhygienic conditions in those places. All in all, it's not something you want to catch.

Typhus is different to what was known as The Black Death. That was popular also, but was much worse. I won't go into details, as you may have just finished eating, but it involved black boils, hence the name. Its main symptoms were a fever and fits of sneezing, and some say it's the origin of the nursery rhyme, 'Ring a Ring o' Roses', and its line about *'Atishoo, Atishoo, all fall down'*.

History books say that two holly trees were planted here, one on either side of the minister's grave, and local legend says that if they ever touch, the plague will return to Largs, but when I was there, I counted at least three holly trees, amongst other kinds, and all touching each other. Still, I haven't heard of any locals breaking out in boils or having bits drop off, but then, they might keep quiet about it - well, wouldn't you?

Quite how all this makes the Rev Smith a prophet, beats me.

HOW TO GET THERE
Heading north out of town on the A78, turn right onto the signposted Brisbane Glen road. Exactly half a mile on the left outside the town limits, go through a small iron gate with a cross and 'Prophet's Grave' sign on it, just after Laigh Middleton House, the one with the posh conservatory.
There's no car park, so be sensible. Follow the grassy path for a couple of hundred yards, towards the shore.

OPENING TIMES

Don't go at night - it's dark.

CHARGES

Free

2
Inverclyde, Scottish National Sports Centre
Burnside, Largs KA30 8RW
Phone 01475 674666 Fax: 01475 674720
Email: johnkent@sportsscotland.org.uk
Website: www.national-sports-centre.com

Set in its own grounds in the hills behind Largs, this is an exceptionally well equipped sports and conference centre, and there is residential accommodation for up to 100 delegates. Here, many of Scotland's national squads train, so you may run into the national football team in training.

If you see them, you have the permission of the whole country to give them a few tips!

The Centre is also a venue for various national and international championship competitions. It's run by Sportscotland for activities and training in gymnastics, volleyball, basketball, badminton, weight training, and other sports, including fly fishing. There's a sports hall, health suite, and squash courts.

Day or residential courses are available too, and the badminton courts are available on a 'casual' basis. Two or four-day golfing tuition holidays are also available.

Phone for details.

HOW TO GET THERE

Largs is on the A78 in North Ayrshire.
Heading north out of town, turn right, following the signposted Inverclyde Sports Centre/Brisbane Glen road just past Vikingar.
Trains run from Glasgow or Ayr to Largs.

OPENING TIMES

Dependant on activity. Phone for details.

CHARGES

Variable, dependant on activity. Phone for details.

3

Vikingar !

Barrfields, Greenock Road, Largs.
Phone: 01475 689777   Fax: 01475 689444
Website: www.vikingar.co.uk

The "**!**" is entirely appropriate, as this is an incredible multimedia attraction, its theme being the Viking invasions of Scotland. Storytellers in Viking garb guide you around and explain everyday life in a recreation of a typical Viking homestead. They'll show you Viking domestic items and weapons, and will also introduce you to Odin, father of all the Viking Gods. You can revisit the aftermath of the Scots v Vikings Battle of Largs of 1263, as 'Egil' tells the story of his family on a five-screen show. (See also entry, 'Pencil Monument')

This interesting presentation is one of the best of its type I've seen, and comes complete with lights, sounds and even smells, for Valhalla's sake!

In the same building is the Pavilion theatre/cinema, with a changing programme of visiting productions and films, a modern family swimming pool and fitness suite, and soft play area for the little ones.

As if that wasn't enough, there's the gift shop, the Winter Garden Café, and the Theatre Bar with its great outlook to the Firth of Clyde and the islands.

Throughout the year, there's a changing list of themed events, from rune reading and saga telling, to crafts and Viking feasts, as well as things for kids like theatre workshops, art activities, and Viking-type games (pillaging, burning, sacking ....only kidding!) All facilities are accessible to wheelchair users, and there is a written account of the main exhibits for the deaf.

Oh, and in case you were wondering, 'Vikingar' is the Viking word for Viking.

Scottish Tourist Board commended.

HOW TO GET THERE

Vikingar! is within walking distance of the town centre, on the right as you go north on the A78.
There's a large grassy area and a replica Viking Longship in front of the building, so you can't miss it.
Trains run from Glasgow or Ayr.

OPENING TIMES

April-September 10.30-6 daily
October-March 10.30-4 daily

CHARGES

Adults £££. Children 4-15yrs/OAP ££.
Family ticket (2 adults + 2 children,
or 1 adult + 3 children) ££££.
There are also discounts for Council Leisure
Card holders, and pre-booked parties.

4
Nardini's
The Esplanade, Largs
Tel: 01475 674555
Website: www.nardini.co.uk

This café is worth a mention and a visit, being so famous throughout the West of Scotland and probably far beyond that, as indeed is their ice cream.

It remains one of the few surviving Art Deco examples of the Golden Age of Scotland's seaside of the 1930's. Even today, one can easily imagine a dinner-suited Palm Court orchestra, gently sawing away in the corner. Scores of thousands have sat in the creaky wicker chairs at the glass-topped wicker tables, have worked their way through a Knickerbocker Glory crowned with Italian double dairy ice cream and Maraschino cherries, and have listened to the hiss and roar of various generations of cappuccino maker. Their ice cream is delicious, and is now on general sale at many outlets throughout Scotland. Nardini's is part of the memory and folklore of countless West of Scotland day trippers, courting couples, and genteel Largs ladies.
Not a great deal has changed over the years - even the ashtrays look the same as I always remember them, the tiled walls in the toilets still have that cracked glazed finish, and the restaurant's decor in still very much in the original style.

Unfortunately though, the prices are trendily modern, so if you're on a tight budget, it's not somewhere you'll be able to visit every day. Still, you should go at least once. Take away some fudge or hand made chocolates or delicious home baking as a souvenir.

On a warm summer evening, it's worth waiting for an outside table to watch the sun set over Arran, and to pretend you're on the Mediterranean somewhere.
Daniella and Peter, members of the family, are now fairly well known actors, having several quality TV and film roles to their names. Peter is also a singer/songwriter of some repute.

HOW TO GET THERE

It's in the central part of town, on the main road right on the promenade opposite the public car park, and next to a large red sandstone church.
Trains run from Glasgow or Ayr.

OPENING TIMES
Early 'til late.

CHARGES
On the high side, but it's worth it for a treat.

5
Largs Museum
Kirkgate House, Manse Court, Largs KA30 8AW.
Tel: 01475 687081
Website link from: www.northayrshiremuseums.org.uk

This small museum has a fine collection of artefacts of everyday life of the past, photographs of old Largs, a library of local books and other publications, and examples of traditional Ayrshire crafts such as embroidery, crockery and Mauchline boxware (see entry, 'Burns House, Mauchline'), and all of which are long gone.

There are also collections of items relating to life during the two World Wars - flags, posters, uniforms, gasmasks, newspapers, etc. All the exhibits have been collected by the local historical society. There is a special section covering the exploits of the Navy vessel, HMS Largs, which was used as a convoy escort during the last War, and was also involved in many Wartime Naval operations.

Looking at old photographs of a town other than your own may sound uninteresting, but it can be fascinating.
If you study them carefully, looking at items such as dress, transport, or even advertising in shop windows, you can often find clues to learn quite a bit about the day-to-day life of those times, and children can have fun making up stories about the people and places they see in the photos. If you're forced to stay indoors on rainy days, this game can keep them occupied for a good while.

If you're interested in ancient history, there's a good leaflet available here, describing and detailing Neolithic sites in the area.

There are explanatory displays and disabled access, and they are also the key holders for the adjacent Skelmorlie Aisle (see next entry). It's unique and beautiful, and is worth seeing.

HOW TO GET THERE

Largs is on the A78 in the north of Ayrshire.
In the centre of the town, Manse Court is off Main Street, by The George pub, between the railway station and the pier.

Trains run from Glasgow or Ayr.

OPENING TIMES

June-September,
2-5 p.m. daily,
or by arrangement.

CHARGES

Free

6
Skelmorlie Aisle
Entrance in Manse Court, Largs
Owned by Historic Scotland
Tel: 0131 668 8800

A fairly important historical relic, and unique in Scotland, the aisle was originally a small side chapel of the old Parish Church, now demolished, so it now stands on its own.

Built in Italian Renaissance style in 1636 by Sir Robert Montgomerie of Skelmorlie for himself and his wife Dame Margaret Douglas, they lie together under an incredible stone mausoleum in the shape of a triumphal arch. There are beautiful and intricate carvings of fruits, flowers, cherubs and animals, as well as a skull and an hourglass, symbols of mortality.

The chapel has a magnificent barrel-vaulted timber ceiling of the same period, the paintings depicting details of biblical text and characters, signs of the zodiac, the Montgomerie coats of arms, and the four seasons, including a summer view of the town with the old church before demolition.

The key is in the adjacent Largs Museum. Just ask, and they'll be delighted to open it for you, and will give you as much time as you want to look around. You can sign the visitor's book and leave your comments.

Previous visitors have described it as, *"beautiful, amazing, breathtaking, fascinating, a real treasure, extraordinary"* and they're not wrong.

The surrounding graveyard contains the tomb of Sir Thomas Makdougall Brisbane, born in the town in 1773, and who came to be Governor of New South Wales, Australia. He was a noted soldier and astronomer, and when a penal colony in Queensland under his command became a free settlement in 1842, the city was named in his honour.

Also here are the flat stones which formed a Neolithic grave of around 2000 BC, discovered near an even older one in Douglas Park. The tomb contained the skeleton of a member of the early Bronze Age 'Beaker' people. (See entry, 'Haylie Chambered Tomb').

HOW TO GET THERE	**OPENING TIMES**
As for Largs Museum (see previous entry). The Aisle is next door.	April-September, 2-5pm, daily. **CHARGES** Free

The Christian Heritage Museum
Mackerston Place, Largs
Tel: 01475 687320

This museum, part of a modern Benedictine Monastery, details the history of Monastic life in Britain and South West Scotland, from Roman times to the present day. Informative, descriptive panels explain every stage of a monk's daily life.

There are examples of the 'illumination' of manuscripts - the highly decorative inking of religious written material - and details of the subjects a monk would study, the work he would do around the monastery, religious music, and other monkly minutiae.

On display are Monastic crafts and silverware, scale models of ancient monasteries, a reconstruction of a typical monk's 'cell' and his daily itinerary, and a beautiful collection of richly embroidered priests' vestments from France and Dumfries Priory.

Home baking and other refreshments are served in the tea room, chanting or non-chanting.

HOW TO GET THERE

Largs is on the A78 in the north of Ayrshire.
Mackerston Place is south of the pier on the seafront, opposite the putting green.

Trains run from Glasgow or Ayr.

OPENING TIMES

April to September, 2-5 p.m., or by prior arrangement, if you'll pardon the pun. (Prior, monastery - get it? Oh, please yourself.)

CHARGES

Free

Right:
Haylie Chambered Tomb which can be seen at Douglas Park in Largs is over 5,000 years old. For details see chapter 8.

Haylie Chambered Tomb
Douglas Park, Largs

This ancient Neolithic burial chamber, or *cromlech,* is within Douglas Park at the foot of Castlehill. At one time, it was covered in stones forming a cairn, and was called Margaret's Law, a *law* being a rounded, conical hill. It comprises four large flat stones on their edges to make walls, and one large flat stone on the top for the lid. This type of structure is called a *proto megalith,* and the tomb has been dated to before 3000 BC.

I'll repeat that, this time in bold print and underlined - **3000 BC,** that's five <u>thousand</u> years old.

That makes it about the same age as the world-renowned Skara Brae Neolithic settlement in Orkney, and probably older than the Great Pyramid of Giza in Egypt. When discovered by a local farmer in 1772, the tomb was found to contain bits of pottery, now lost, and several skeletons, most of which were destroyed by inexperienced handling. It was only in 1954 that a formal excavation was carried out, when remains of a fire, some flint scrapers, and two skeletons were found, one probably female. Neolithic people lived in very small communities, and were farmers and hunters, but little else is known about their way of life. The tomb is about 15 feet long (about 5 metres), but now only the basic shape is visible, even though it's covered in brambles and weeds.

Another grave was discovered in 1906, very close to this one. Inside was a pottery jar and one skeleton, buried in a sitting position. This was enough to identify the occupant as a member of the early Bronze Age 'Beaker' people of around 2000 BC. They buried their dead like this in the belief that when the warrior awoke in the Next World, he would be able to grab his weapons which were buried with him, and spring immediately into action. The stones which formed this chamber are kept in a corner of the old Largs graveyard, next to Largs Museum. (See entry. 'Skelmorlie Aisle')

At the top of Castlehill is the site of an Iron Age fort, vaguely and frustratingly dated to somewhere between 500 BC and 200 AD. Apparently, several other cairns were discovered in this area, but were destroyed during road making in the 1700's. Very few records of them exist, so no-one knows for sure what kind of people built the fort. Obviously, though, this was a very popular area in prehistoric times. Unfortunately, there are no plaques or explanations at the site, but there's a good leaflet available in Largs Museum.

HOW TO GET THERE

Douglas Park is on Irvine Road, on the left leaving Largs on the main A78 south.
You can drive through the green iron gates of the Bowling Club, and go part way up the hill to the right of the gardens behind the tennis courts, then it's a short walk to the site.
Trains run from Glasgow or Ayr.

OPENING TIMES

Access at any time within park opening hours

CHARGES

Free

9
Haylie Brae Picnic Area
near Largs

This is a perfect stopping-off point with fantastic views over the Firth of Clyde to Great and Little Cumbrae, Arran, Kintyre, and northwards to the hills and mountains of Argyll. There's a barrier across the entrance, so if you're in a vehicle substantially bigger than an ordinary car, you won't get under it. The barrier's to stop caravans parking there overnight, or even over a fortnight, but it's hard luck if you're in a camper van. Still, once you do get in, there are several picnic tables to choose from. There are big yellow litter bins as well, so please use them, or take your rubbish home.

From the car park, there is a short uphill path to a viewpoint plaque, telling you that you can see as far south as Ailsa Craig, a distance of around 38 miles (61 km). There's also a small reservoir nearby, but fishing, picnics and bathing are all prohibited, and you should keep an eye on youngsters.

We needn't have perfect Summer weather to get epic sunsets in this part of Scotland, indeed, many of the very best are in Autumn and Spring, and this is an ideal location to see them, so I make no apologies for its inclusion in this book.

HOW TO GET THERE Leave Largs on A760 Kilbirnie road at the south end of town, and follow the picnic area signs to the top of Haylie Brae, a twisting uphill road through the trees.	**OPENING TIMES** Accessible at all reasonable times **CHARGES** Free

Right: Spectacular views of the Firth of Clyde islands - like this one of Arran with its snowy peaks - can be seen from several points along the Ayrshire coastline.

10
Largs Yacht Haven
Irvine Road, Largs Ayrshire, KA30 8EZ.
(or 55° 46.42N 004° 51.45W if you're sailing there!)
Tel: 01475 675333. Fax: 01475 672245
Email:largsyh@aol.com
Websites: www.yachthavens.com   www.largssc.co.uk
www.scottishsailinginstitute.com

This is a large, modern complex, home to Largs Sailing Club and the Scottish Sailing Institute.

International sailing events are sometimes staged from here, and if you're a boat owner, it's an ideal base for cruising the waters of the Clyde and beyond to Ireland. The marina's shops, restaurant and bars are open to casual visitors, of course.

There's a well-stocked ship's chandler with literally everything from a needle to an anchor, an engineer and boat sales, or you can book a charter or lessons, or arrange diving and sea angling trips. Drop in for a snack or a meal and to pick up details of what's available and prices. There are always boats for sale, of course, or you can just dream about them until your Lottery numbers come up.

It's not easy to study the boats closely, as locked gates discourage casual visitors from wandering around the pontoons, understandably.

If you're a sailor of any description, you'll love it here.

There is another Yacht Haven, owned by the same parent company, at Troon, just north of Ayr. It's not as modern as Largs, though, and its facilities are on a smaller scale.

HOW TO GET THERE

It's situated on the A78, on the right, just south of the town limits. Follow the signs.
Turn off the road and go over the steep bridge over the railway.

OPENING TIMES

The retail outlets keep shop hours. Bar and restaurant open 'til late.

CHARGES
Free to look around.

11
The Pencil Monument
Off Irvine Road, Largs

Built in 1912, it's a tall, slim, but empty cylindrical stone tower with a pointed roof, hence the name.

It commemorates the Battle of Largs of October 1263, when the Scots, under Alexander III, trounced the Viking invaders of King Haakon's army in this area. Some say though, that the annual Autumn storms which Alexander had held out for, combined with the ill health of the Norse king, had more to do with the victory than the fighting talents of the Scottish forces, but who cares - we won.

Strangely, the invaders claimed victory, too, and apparently, some Norwegians still won't accept the battle didn't go their way. Anyway, that's what Magnus Magnusson says, and he should know.

There had been Viking raids on Britain for generations, of course, but finally, following this fierce fracas, the formerly fearless fighting fleet was floored, and they fled fast, having run out of 'f's. They rowed non-stop until they got to the main island of Orkney, a distance of some 450 miles (724 km). The last three were agony - they were over land.

King Haakon's cough was not improving, though, and he took to his bed. (Hackin' cough - get it? Oh, please yourself!) His friends decided that, to cheer him up, they would read aloud to him from the unabridged version of the Complete Sagas Of All The Norse Kings Ever Since The Year Dot. However, this was so uninteresting with not many laughs and no pictures to look at, that Haakon's condition worsened. His eyes crossed, he started dribbling, and he died with his leg up, probably from mind-mangling boredom. Spookily, later Sagas, detailed written histories, say that *en route* to the battle, the fleet witnessed a solar eclipse, which the onboard Watcher of the Skies had interpreted to be an omen of the King's impending doom. I don't know what Viking for *"I told you so"* is, but I bet someone said it.

After Haakon's death, his successor realised he should have called the doctor much earlier, decided he couldn't be bothered with all that fighting again, and agreed to negotiate peace terms. The Scots offered the Vikings 4000 marks to go away forever, and 100 marks annually to spend on sweets, and the deal was made, leading to the ending of Viking territorial claims on mainland Scotland. Incidentally, it appears that not many payments were made, possibly the start of that clichéd rumour about Scots being mean!

Before he left the area, Haakon was granted permission to bury his dead on nearby Little Cumbrae island, where some Viking-type relics have been found.

The battle is a good excuse to have a Viking Festival in Largs in late August and September, when amongst other events, there is a recreation of a typical Viking village along the prom, where you can visit and see what everyday Viking life was like.

There's also a big parade, during which frightening hairy figures in big winged helmets and dressed in sheepskins march up and down the main street, swinging enormous lethal-looking axes and swords, and roaring 'Ha-HAA!!' loudly at passers-by...even the <u>men</u> in the parade do the same!

The closing highlight of the Festival is at the Pencil, where there's a re-enactment of the battle, the burning of a replica Viking ship, and most spectacularly, a **fantastic** fireworks display, easily the best in the area, and well worth the wait and the midgie bites. The best place to see it is from the beach, where the explosions and flashes are reflected in the water.

The pyrotechnics are carefully placed, so it appears as if they are being fired from out of the top of the monument!

If you want the full,unexpurgated 1889 version of this story, go to: www.maybole.org/history/ Books/legends/kinghaco.htm on the Internet.

See also the entry *Alexander III* in the Anti-Confusion Ancient History Chapter.

HOW TO GET THERE

On the A78 south out of Largs, you can't really miss it. It's on the beach beyond the football pitches and railway line on the right as you go round the corner and down the hill, just leaving the town limits. Follow the signs to Largs Yacht Haven, park there, and walk along the short shore path.
On the way, there are picnic tables and rock pools. A lot of people walk their dogs here, so watch your feet.

OPENING TIMES

Since it's only viewable from the outside, access is free at any reasonable time.

CHARGES

Free

12
Kelburn Castle and Country Centre
Fairlie, Ayrshire KA29 0BE
Phone: 01475 568685 Fax: 01475 568121
Website: www.kelburncountrycentre.com

Dating from the 13th Century, but much added to over the centuries, this has been the family home of the Boyle family, the Earls of Glasgow, for more than two hundred years.

There is long-standing but friendly rivalry between Kelburn and Traquair House in the Borders as to which is the oldest, continuously-inhabited stately home in Scotland. Kelburn claims the prize as the oldest, continuously-inhabited-by-the-same-family stately home, but Traquair may have different ways of aiming at the same goalposts!

Whatever is the pedantic truth, Kelburn has exotic gardens, and natural woodlands and pathways to waterfalls and gorges, leading to great views over the Firth of Clyde.

The grounds contain a huge Weeping Larch, covering half an acre, and the tallest Monterey Pine in Scotland. There's loads for kids to do - Adventure Course, Commando Assault Course, Adventure Playground, the Wooden Stockade, pets corner, horse riding, pony trekking, and indoor soft play area, as well as a museum, crafts and gift shop, and licenced café in an old byre. (Mercifully, they've got rid of the smell.)

The Secret Forest is a major attraction, with paths and overhead walkways cutting through the thick woods to exciting fantasy areas like The Castle With No Entrance, Gingerbread House, Maze Of The Green Man, Crocodile Swamp, and The Chinese Pagoda.

Birds of prey and falconry displays can be seen May to September, but check in advance for details.

There is a widely varying, ever-changing programme of events within the Park, including seasonal children's entertainment, outdoor concerts, Ranger activities and guided walks, but phone for details of these too. Plan to spend most of the day here.

Scottish Tourist Board Commended.

HOW TO GET THERE

Kelburn is on the A78, just south of Largs. Alternatively, take the train to Largs and get the free minibus from the station at 11.45 and 1.45 every weekend, from early May to late August, and every day in July and August.
The last bus back to Largs leaves Kelburn at 4.30pm.

OPENING TIMES

Easter - end October, all attraction and facilities, 10-6 daily, Secret Forest from 12 noon.
Castle - July-Sept, guided tours in afternoons only.
Out of season - grounds only, 11-5 daily, except Xmas Day, Boxing Day & New Year's Day.

CHARGES

Adults £££ , all concessions ££.
Castle tours, £ extra, but confirm availability in advance.
Entry fees out of season - Adults ££, concessions £.

13
Clyde Muirshiel Country Park

Headquarters - Barnbrock Farm, Kilbarchan, Renfrewshire PA10 2PZ
Tel: 01505 614791 Fax: 01505 813605
Email: enquiries@muirshiel.sol.co.uk
Website: www.scottishpark.com

This is one of Scotland's four Regional Parks, covering over 100 square miles (160 square km), and attracting over 4 million visitors per year. There are about 100 working farms and over 150 miles (240 km) of paths and trails within its boundaries. Only parts of it are in Ayrshire, the rest in neighbouring Renfrewshire, but because it covers adjacent areas, it would make no sense to leave bits of it out of this book, so I've detailed all the Park's six outdoor properties within its boundaries. There are woods, moors, farms, glens, parks, lochs and coast, all within about 20 miles (32 km) or so from Glasgow.

This huge area supports over 160 species of birds, with animals and wild plants aplenty. The woods have roe deer, foxes, badgers, squirrels, pheasants, shrews and voles, the lochs have ducks, geese, fish and even otters, and the moors are home to rare orchids and several species of birds of prey. There are Iron Age hill forts, Medieval houses, and fine examples of Victorian civil engineering, as well as plenty opportunities for active pursuits such as sailing, canoeing, hill-walking, windsurfing, golf, archery and fishing.

Properties are **Barnbrock Farm; Cornalees Bridge Visitor Centre; Lunderston Bay Picnic & Play Area; Castle Semple Water Park & Visitor Centre; Lochwinnoch RSPB Nature Reserve,** and **Muirshiel Visitor Centre.** (Vikingar! and Kelburn Castle & Country Park in Largs are officially part of the Park too, but they're detailed on previous pages.)

There is a huge range of activities for all ages and interests every weekend and some weekdays, and you should get the comprehensive leaflet, detailing a whole season's events at all locations. Many events are free, others cost just a pound or two. All centres are detailed on the following pages.

There's nothing to 'see' at Barnbrock Farm as it's really just the Park's HQ, but it does have sheilings - A-framed huts -, a campsite for tents only, toilets, kitchen and laundry, picnic area, and access to nearby Locherwood Community Woodland.

Scottish Tourist Board Commended.

HOW TO GET THERE

Kilbarchan is 3 miles (4.8km) north of Lochwinnoch on the B786.
Trains run from Glasgow and Ayr to Lochwinnoch, but there is no public transport to the site.

OPENING TIMES
Barnbrock Farm offices, Monday-Friday 9-4.30, all year.
Campsite open daily in summer.

CHARGES
Camping, adults ££, child/concession £.

13a
Cornalees Bridge Visitor Centre
Loch Thom, by Inverkip, Renfrewshire PA16 9LX
Tel: 01475 521458
Email: enquiries@muirshiel.sol.co.uk
Website: www.scottishpark.com

The Centre sits at the side of Loch Thom in the moors and hills above Greenock, and it's odd to think that you're just a few short miles from what used to be some of the mightiest shipbuilding yards in the world. Fishing in the loch is by permit only, so ask at the fisherman's hut for details.

There is a marked trail down the side of Kip Water through Greenock Cut, a Victorian aqueduct 5 miles (8 km) long, built in 1825 to supply drinking water and water power to the town and its industries. The designer was Robert Thom, and this impressive piece of engineering cost the grand sum of £51,000, only three times over budget! But the town was so pleased with it, they named the loch after him. The Cut was awarded Ancient Monument status in 1972, but neglect over many years has caused a partnership between the Country Park management and other local bodies applying for Lottery funding to renovate and restore it and the Visitor Centre.

Sheilhill Glen is a woodland designated as an S.S.S.I. - Site of Special Scientific Interest (try saying that after a few drinks!). You will see woodland and moorland birds and, if you're lucky, Roe deer. There are great views over the Clyde estuary at the top of the trail, and unsurprisingly, evidence has been found here of Roman roads, signal posts and forts. The path continues through Kelly Cut, another aqueduct, before finishing back at the Centre, a circular walk of about 7 miles (11 km). In the Centre, there are local and natural history exhibits, indoor environmentally-themed games, details of navigation and orienteering courses, children's summer activities, guided walks and Ranger service, explanatory slide show, gift shop and picnic areas. There are toilets and access for the disabled.

If you're travelling to Cornalees or Lunderston Bay from Lochwinnoch or Muirshiel, you'll be on the B788. Just as you begin to descend towards Greenock, stop in the small layby and you'll be rewarded with an incredible view of the Clyde estuary, Gare Loch, Loch Long, Holy Loch, Greenock, Gourock, Helensburgh, Dunoon, Ben Lomond and other mountains of the southern Highlands and inner islands. Make sure you've got film in your camera, and choose a good day.

HOW TO GET THERE

The quickest way is to leave the A78, halfway between Largs and Greenock, a little north of Inverkip village. Take the signposted road to Loch Thom, just before the IBM factory complex. There is another way through the village but you would need the help of Global Positioning Satellite and a team of local Sherpas.
The nearest railway station is Inverkip.

OPENING TIMES

12-4 daily in summer, weekends only in winter

CHARGES

Free

13b
Lunderston Bay Picnic & Play Area
by Inverkip
Tel: 01475 521129
Email: enquiries@muirshiel.sol.co.uk
Website: www.scottishpark.com

More than half a million people a year visit this unspoilt sand and pebble beach on the coast of the Clyde estuary, and it's a great place for picnics on warm days.

Recently, it was awarded the yellow Seaside Award flag, meaning that the water and the beach meet stringent European Union standards of cleanliness and safety.

There are incredible panoramic views from Arran in the south to the Cowal peninsula, and beyond to the mountains of Argyll and Jura. There is a large picnicking area where dogs are not allowed, so the grass should be 'safe'. A few yards away is a children's adventure playground where, again, dogs are not allowed.

You can do beach walks, watch the marine birds, look for wild flowers, or skiddle about in rock pools.

In season, there are guided tours of the immediate area, children's activities, and Ranger service.

Disabled access and toilets.

HOW TO GET THERE

Lunderston Bay is on the A770 coast road, off the A78, between Largs and Gourock, just north of Inverkip.
Nearest railway station is Inverkip.

OPENING TIMES

Open daily all year from 10 am.

CHARGES

Free

Castle Semple Water Park & Visitor Centre
Lochlip Road, Lochwinnoch, Renfrewshire PA12 4EA.
Tel: 01505 842882
Email: enquiries@muirshiel.sol.co.uk

Castle Semple Loch is a small loch in attractive surroundings, offering sailing, canoeing, windsurfing and fishing, with sailing craft and mountain bikes for hire at selected times. You can also receive tuition in canoeing, dinghy sailing and archery.

Attractions at the Visitor Centre include local and natural history displays, lecture room, guided tours of the area, showers for those who get wet during the sailing, Ranger service, gift shop and picnic areas. There's also an interesting twelve-minute film which will tell you everything you need to know about the Park. There's full access for the disabled, and a cafeteria for refreshments.

Formerly part of Castle Semple estate, the nearby Parkhill Wood has attractive woodland walks and a rebuilt grotto.

Historical landmarks around the town include Peel Castle of 1550 (1550 - that's ten to four isn't it? Oh, never mind....), and the ruins of the Collegiate Church of around 1504. (Won't do that joke again.....)

HOW TO GET THERE

From Largs take the A760 to Lochwinnoch. From Ayr take the A78 to Kilwinning, then the A737 for Glasgow. The Centre is at the loch side in Lochwinnoch. From Glasgow take the M8 west. At the airport, turn off on to the A737 to Lochwinnoch, and follow the signs.
Trains run from Glasgow and Ayr to Lochwinnoch, but the station is 1 mile outside the town. Despite it being a small, unmanned station, trains do stop on Sundays.

OPENING TIMES

1 April-end Oct - 10-8
or dusk if earlier.
Nov-March - 10-4 daily.

CHARGES

Free

13d
Lochwinnoch RSPB Nature Reserve
Largs Road, Lochwinnoch PA12 4JF
Tel: 01505 842663   Fax: 01505 843026
Email: lochwinnoch@rspb.org.uk
Website: www.scottishpark.com

As if you didn't know, RSPB is a charity, and stands for the Royal Society for the Protection of Birds. This area is one of the few remaining low-lying wetland environments in this part of the country, making it an S.S.S.I. - Site of Special Scientific Interest. That means it's a protected area for the study and the conservation of birds and mammals on and around Castle Semple Loch and neighbouring Barr Loch, although why neither is called Loch Winnoch, I don't know. Three main areas can be studied - the loch of course, with its collection of ducks, swans, geese, herons and all manner of water birds; the marshes, containing many examples of wet-loving plants and grasses and their associated winged residents; and the woodland areas, with their treecreepers, flycatchers, woodpeckers and even a few Roe deer. The Reserve is proud of its family of otters, which, if you're up early enough, you may see fishing and playing in the loch, and it is also an important breeding site for a dozen or so pairs of Great Crested Grebes, a rare and attractive water bird.

The Visitor Centre has wardens and explanatory displays, charts of the most common birds, and details of their seasons, and you can have free use of binoculars and telescopes. You can also buy teas, coffees and snacks, and the well-stocked shop has souvenirs, some seriously professional telescopes and binoculars for sale, and every bird book you're ever liable to want. You can even join the RSPB here. Upstairs is a viewing tower where you will get even better views of the loch and its residents.

Walk through the trees, with your binoculars to hand of course, to the bird hides, and at any time of the year you are sure to be rewarded with closeup views of birds feeding, nesting, or doing-whatever-it-is-that-birds-do-when-they-think-they're-not-being-watched-by-people-with-binoculars. The main Glasgow to Ayrshire railway line at their backs doesn't seem to bother them, either. Paths and hides are accessible to wheelchairs, although the paths may be muddy in places after rain. In the hides, you will find charts and pictures of the birds you are most likely to see. There are guided walks, craft demonstrations, special events of various types throughout the year, and the Rangers also run environmental classes for schools.

HOW TO GET THERE

From Largs, take the A760. From the A737, take the A760 to Lochwinnoch. Cross the railway bridge, and the Centre is on the right.

It's just opposite the entrance to Lochwinnoch station, and trains stop on Sundays.

OPENING TIMES

Visitor centre, 10-5 daily, all year, except Xmas and New Year. Paths and hides open at all times.

CHARGES

Visitor Centre free.
Trails free to RSPB and Young Ornithologists Club members.
Non members - adults ££, children/concessions £.
Family ticket £££.

18

13e
Muirshiel Visitor Centre
Calder Glen Road, by Lochwinnoch, Renfrewshire PA12 4LB
Tel: 01505 842803
Email: enquiries@muirshiel.sol.co.uk
Website: www.scottishpark.com

Muirshiel's heyday was in Victorian times when it was a large estate, owned by the Conyngham family, and given over to the sporting pleasures of the huntin', shootin', and fishin' fraternity. Nowadays, many not-so-violent activities are on offer, and anyone can join in. The estate, high in the hills, passed into public hands in the 50's, but by that time the house was in such a dangerous condition, demolition was the only option. The Visitor Centre now stands on the site of the house.

Muirshiel should be used as a base for taking different walks in the woods and hills. There are four different walks, each through different areas - the Habitat Trail, and no, you can't buy nice rugs or trendy furniture; the Country Trail; the Waterfall Trail, and guess where that ends up; and the romantically-named Windy Hill Trail, which I assume refers merely to the nice breeze you get up there, and not to the effects of that curry you had last night. All the trails are signposted and colour coded, so you shouldn't get lost, and none of them takes longer than an hour or so from start to finish, unless you really take your time. On the way, there are picnic areas, fresh air and nice views.

The small baryte mine on the estate was opened in the mid 1800's, and continued producing until the 1960's, when the shafts were sealed off. Baryte is a whitish mineral used in paint and paper manufacturing. If you've ever had a barium meal, that's what you were drinking, or maybe you had it, er, 'injected'......! If you're into geology, there are examples of strontianite, calcite, pyrite, quartz and celestine in the area.

This peaceful and relaxing location is rich in archaeological sites, and the botanist and birdwatcher will be in his or her element. Birds of prey are easily spotted, so you should see falcons, harriers and merlins. Orienteering and navigation courses are on offer throughout the season, as are different kinds of country crafts demonstrations like wind chime making, or How To Make Your Own Besom. (They mean those old-fashioned brooms, the kind that witches ride on!)

There are guided tours, Ranger service, explanatory displays, toilets and a gift shop. The Laird's Kitchen serves meals or snacks. Note - dogs are allowed within Muirshiel's boundaries, but not on adjacent privately-owned land.

HOW TO GET THERE

The Centre is about 3 miles (4.8 km) along a single track road off the B786 Lochwinnoch to Kilmacolm road. The nearest railway station is Lochwinnoch.

OPENING TIMES
April-Sept, 12-5 daily.
Oct-March, 12-4 weekends.

CHARGES
Free

14
Hunterston Power Station Visitor Centre
West Kilbride, Ayrshire KA23 9RA
Phone: 0800 838557

Hunterston 'A' station, opened in 1964, is the site of two 150 megawatt nuclear reactors, and was decommissioned in 1990, basically because Scotland was generating more electricity than it could get rid of. It is now ten years or so into a 135-year-long switch off. On your visit, you will find out why it takes so long.

Hunterston 'B', commissioned in 1976, is much larger, is of a different design to the 'A' reactor, and still produces about half of Scotland's power requirements. The tour is designed to explain each stage of the generating and shutdown processes through videos, displays and models. Most areas can be toured with guides who explain everything in unscientific language, and the statistics are very impressive. You also get close-up views of the control room, the reactor, and the huge turbine hall.
If conditions are right, you'll see the waste water boiling up impressively in the sea adjacent to the reactors.

When viewed from the main road at night, the ghostly green lights make the building look like some huge square spaceship, half hiding behind a hill. It's a 'must' for science-minded kids and dads. At the moment, there are suggestions that a new reactor may be built here, but the idea hasn't gone down well with all politicians or conservation groups. If they shut down the 'A' reactor, how come they now need another one, that's what I want to know.

From any clear position along this part of the coast, you will see the ore terminal and the giant cranes. Iron ore for the Scottish steel industry was intended to be unloaded here, and was supposed to be smelted here too, but the furnaces were never lit and no iron was ever produced. Just as well, considering the pollution there would have been.

Its construction more or less coincided with the death of the industry in Scotland, another fine example of a waste of public money! Now, foreign coal is offloaded here, since UK coal production has all but ceased. The enclosed bridge over the road at the entrance to the power station is part of the overhead conveyer belt system, which loads the coal onto railway trucks for delivery to other parts of the country.

HOW TO GET THERE

It's on the A78, south of Largs, between Fairlie and Seamill.
The turnoff is at a large roundabout with trees in the middle and is well signposted with BIG signs, so you'll not miss it.

Nearest train stations are at West Kilbride or Fairlie.

OPENING TIMES

Pre-booked tours only,
Mon-Fri, 09.30-4.30.

CHARGES

No charge, if you'll pardon the pun.
(Charge, electricity - oh, please yourself!)

15
The ATV Adventure Company
Blackshaw Farm, Dalry Road, West Kilbride KA23 9PG
Phone: 01294 823014.
Website: www.atvXtreme.com

Blackshaw Farm is the home of the ATV Adventure Company, which offers quad bike treks, cross country treks starting at around £5 for 6 to 12 year olds, and £20 for a full 1-hour trek for over 12's and parents. If a cross-country trek is not for you, you can take the machine round a closed circuit instead.

The same company also offers clay pigeon shooting, and indoor & outdoor air rifle ranges. They are also geared up for corporate or group events, and can even bring the bikes to you if you have a suitable area, and by that they don't mean a big back garden!
Full safety gear, instruction and wet weather clothing is included in the prices.

HOW TO GET THERE

From the A78 at West Kilbride, take the B781. From the A737 at Dalry, take the B780.

OPENING TIMES
Daylight hours throughout the year.

CHARGES
Variable, depending on requirements.
Check the website or phone for details.

Above:
The Silver Arrow Trophy is awarded to the winner of a morning competition on the same day as "The Papingo Shoot" held each year at Kilwinning Abbey. See chapter 20.

16
West Kilbride Museum
Arthur Street, West Kilbride

This is a small museum set up and run by the West Kilbride Museum Society. It displays a collection of Victorian and Edwardian clothes from the Hunterston Estate costume collection, as well as old toys and household objects from the Victorian age to the War years. Exhibitions change on a regular basis, so you never know what will be on display. Also on display are examples of beautiful Ayrshire lace and embroidery, trade and craft implements, and a recreation of a turn-of-the-century room.

Hunterston Castle, on nearby Hunterston Estate, was built around 1400 by the Hunter family, who still live there, but not the same ones, obviously.
In fact, Hunters have had around 800 years of uninterrupted habitation on this same site, having first built a timber and earth fort.

This stone castle was only about 24' by 21' and 30' high (8 x 7 x 10 m) at first, but has been much extended over the centuries. Originally, it had a moat for defence, and sat in the middle of a swamp, and, like something from The Hound of the Baskervilles, you had to be a member of the family or a trusted servant to know the safe way through.

A charter exists, signed by King Robert II in 1374, officially granting the land to the Hunter family for services rendered. It states that the chief of the Hunter clan must pay the Monarch one silver penny if he visits on the Feast of Pentecost (around the middle of May). For that reason, the Clan Chief keeps some coins of the period in his sock drawer. Well, you can never be over-prepared, can you?

Nowadays, Hunterston Castle is a splendid family home and is the headquarters of the Hunter Clan. If a member, they will help you look up your ancestors, and you can visit by appointment. Non-Clan members can visit on a once-a-year Open Day, or visit the website at www.clanhunter.com

HOW TO GET THERE

West Kilbride is just off the A78 in Fairlie, between Ardrossan and Largs. Go right up to the top of the hill, to where the road levels off. Arthur Street is first on the left. From the A737 at Dalry, take the B780 to West Kilbride. The museum is near the police station, in a North Ayrshire Council building on the corner of Ritchie Street, a continuation of Main Street, and Arthur Street, just off the town's centre.
Hunterston Castle is on a private estate, and is not open to the general public.

OPENING TIMES

Museum
10.30-12.30, 2-4,
Tues, Thurs-Sat,
all year.

CHARGES

Free

17
Portencross Castle and Law Castle
West Kilbride

Two other castles in the immediate West Kilbride area are worth a quick mention, if only for their antiquity. Portencross Castle (from the Gaelic *port na croisse*, port or ferry of the crossing) dates from around 1390, though there was an earlier one on the same site which had been used by Robert the Bruce. The castle's main entrance was, as is usual for this type, one floor up, and the wooden staircase which led to the door would be drawn up during times of danger. Unusually though, there was a second kitchen and entrance on the ground floor level, the reason being that when Robert II would bring troops and servants for a day at the seaside, possibly on their way from Dundonald Castle to Rothesay Castle, they camped around the castle and were fed from this kitchen, leaving the Royal kitchen uncluttered with their wellies or buckets and spades.

Portencross was used as a staging post for the bodies of Scottish kings. Their traditional burial place was the island of Iona, and the body would lie in state here, until suitable transport could be arranged. Around 1660, the incumbent Boyd family moved to newer premises and the castle was taken over by what was wonderfully described as *"fishermen and other inferior tenants"*! All was well until one dark stormy night in 1739, when a fierce gale blew the roof off, a fate which often befalls properties in this area, even today! Recently, Scottish Power bought the castle from the family which owned it - a family called Adams, and no, I will not make jokes about that - and have paid for some restoration work. It is known that several Stewart Kings used the castle, as documents signed there are still in existence, so it was an important place. God alone knows why, as, being right on the edge of the sea, it must have been thoroughly miserable in the teeth of a howling winter gale. However, for sunny days, there are picnic tables, a good rocky shore for guddling about, and nice views of the coast. The castle is not normally open, but it's been for sale for a few years, so perhaps someone will restore it.

Law Castle stands above West Kilbride on Law Hill. It dates from around 1468, and was built for Princess Mary, sister of James III of Scotland. It was designed not so much as a castle, but more as an elegant home, with proper windows, fireplaces, and plastered interior walls. She had married Thomas Boyd, one of the Boyds of Kilmarnock (see entry 'Dean Castle and Country Park'), the first Earl of Arran, but following accusations of treason and treachery, the Earl and his father fled Scotland. Mary, with an eye on the main chance and wishing to keep her nice house, divorced Thomas and married Lord Hamilton, who coincidentally, had just been named as the new Earl of Arran! No flies on her, then.

After the death of the last incumbents in the early 1600's, squatters and probably some of the aforementioned *"inferior tenants"* moved in. Wouldn't you just know it - a gale blew the roof off, and that was the end of them. It is now again in private hands, and at least on the outside, is in a high degree of preservation with new roughcasting and nice magnolia paint. It's a shame that it's not open to visitors, but note that it's a **private** dwelling, so **don't** go staring in the windows!

HOW TO GET THERE
Portencross is at the end of the narrow B7048, signposted from the A78 at Seamill. Law Castle is on the hill behind the railway station in West Kilbride. Go up Law Brae.

North Ayrshire Museum
Manse Street, Saltcoats
Tel: 01294 464174
Email: namuseum@globalnet.co.uk
Website: www.northayrshiremuseums.org.uk
Website for Saltcoats: www.visitsaltcoats.com

This interesting museum is housed in a former church of 1744, and its many displays reflect the civic, rural, and maritime history of the area, as well as having sections on local archaeology, and the town's former glory as a seaside resort. The life of Saltcoats resident Betsy Miller, who in 1847, became the first registered female sea captain, is commemorated also.

There is a reconstruction of the inside of your typical Victorian cottage, examples of everyday household items of the past, a local Bronze Age stone coffin, and the town's old hand-operated fire engine.

There is also a beautiful copy of the famous Hunterston Brooch, found in at the bottom of a cliff in 1826 near Hunterston Power Station further up the coast. It's a magnificent and priceless silver, gold and amber item measuring about five inches (12.5cm) across, made around the 8th Century. Perhaps it was lost by one of the Viking chiefs around the time of the Battle of Largs in 1293. (See entry, 'Pencil Monument') The name 'Malbride' or 'Malbrigda', possibly its owner's name, is inscribed on the back in Runes, the name given to Viking script. Apparently, bones were also found nearby, so perhaps he fell off, or was pushed off, the cliff. The original is now in the Museum of Scotland in Edinburgh, and a wonderful object it is too. It's a perfect example of several different styles of decoration, including Viking, Celtic and Anglo-Saxon, and is displayed in such a way that you can get very close to it and see both sides. If in Edinburgh, it's well worth seeing. Note that, when they purchased it in 1891, they paid the bargain price of £500!

A recent addition to the Saltcoats display is the headstone of the Poe family, rescued from the former churchyard on the site. This is the same Poe as the writer, Edgar Allan. His family lived in the area, and the young Edgar spent part of his boyhood here and in nearby Irvine, before emigrating to America.

There's a childrens' activity and discovery area, as well as guided tours, explanatory displays, gift shop, reference section and photographic collection. Full disabled access and toilets.

HOW TO GET THERE

Saltcoats is on the A78, 12 miles (19 km) south of Largs. Trains run from Glasgow and Ayr. The museum is just off Hamilton Street near the town centre.

OPENING TIMES

All year, Mon, Tues, Thurs, Fri, & Sat, 10-1, 2-5. Closed also on Public Holidays.

CHARGES

Free

19
Dalgarven Mill, Kilwinning
Dalry Road, Kilwinning KA13 6PN
Tel: 01294 552448
Website link from: www.northayrshiremuseums.org.uk
Website for Kilwinning: www.kilwinning.org

It's thought that there's been a mill on this site for about six hundred years, being established by the monks of nearby Kilwinning Abbey, but the present building dates from about 1620, with restoration following a major fire in 1880.

For a long time, it was unused and pretty much a ruin, but the current owner inherited it from his family and has carefully and lovingly brought it back to life.

Milling equipment has been restored, though at the time of writing, the big water wheel needs further work unfortunately, and isn't working.

The building now has a multi-purpose use, and on several floors, it houses a Country Life Museum of local farming and domestic life (a lot more interesting than it might sound), and a changing costume collection of local 18th and 19th Century clothing, old embroidery and Ayrshire lace, including incidentally, my family Christening robe!

The top floor contains the recreated mill owner's house and mill worker's cottage. On the ground floor, the tearoom sells light meals, snacks, souvenirs, and a delicious selection of home-baking, including sinful but wonderful chocolate cake!

Opposite the mill is The Byre, a small Antiques and Collectables shop.

Scottish Tourist Board Commended.

HOW TO GET THERE

Situated on the A737 between Dalry and Kilwinning, at the small hamlet of Dalgarven.

OPENING TIMES

Easter-end of October, Mon-Sat 10-5, Sunday 11-5.
Winter period, Wed-Sun 11-4
Groups welcome, but please phone to book first.

CHARGES

Adults ££, concessions £

Kilwinning Abbey

Main Street, Kilwinning
Correspondence to:
North Ayrshire Museum, Manse Street, Saltcoats KA21 5AA
Tel /Fax: 01294 464174
Email: namuseum@globalnet.co.uk
Website link from: www.northayrshiremuseums.org.uk
Website for Kilwinning: www.kilwinning.org

The precise origins of this rich Abbey are not known. It was founded around 1184, probably as an act of penance by the English knight and an early Lord of Cunninghame (north Ayrshire), Richard de Morville, for his part in the murder of Archbishop Thomas Becket in Canterbury Cathedral in 1170.

We do know for sure that it was destroyed during the Reformation in the mid-1500's. During its life, it became a large and important complex of many buildings, fields and orchards. It had enormous twin towers, by far the largest structures in the area before or since, but both now long gone. The most substantial original remnant which remains is the south transept gable, with its pointed narrow windows.

On a nearby doorway, heavily worn but still visible, are two carved figures, thought to represent Adam and Eve. Dominating the town, and still a landmark for many miles around, is a square clock tower of 1815, around 120 feet (36.5m) high - high enough, but not as tall as the original medieval twin towers were. There are explanatory description boards in the grounds.

Each Summer on a Saturday afternoon in early June, the Ancient Society of Kilwinning Archers holds its Papingo shoot at the tower, indeed, the tower was built partly to replace an earlier one destroyed by lightning, and partly due to pressure from the archers to continue an ancient tradition. ('Papingo', with the emphasis on the second 'p', is the Scots variation of the archaic English word *popinjay* or *parrot.*) The Society claims to be the oldest in the UK, if not the world, and dates back to around 1488.

In the competition, a wooden bird about six inches (16 cm) across (the Papingo), but originally a live parrot, sits on the end of a long pole sticking out from the top of the tower, 120 ft (44m) from the ground. The archers shoot at it from ground level, and the first to knock the bird off its perch (and remember, this started in the 15th Century, long before Monty Python!) wins a silver replica of the clock tower.

The winner of a morning target shoot is presented with the magnificent Silver Arrow of 1724, on permanent display in Kilwinning library. If you don't believe a single word of this, think shame on yourself, and read Sir Walter Scott's novel, *Old Mortality,* as the competition features in its opening chapters.

The tower is now a Heritage Centre, and contains exhibits relating to the Papingo shoot, and other details of various aspects of the long history of the town. They also have some census records dating from the late 19th Century, and information and photographs of the life and works of Robert Service.

Known as The Yukon Poet, he spent four years of his childhood in the town, but emigrated to Canada in 1895 where he was inspired by the Gold Rush to write such classics as *The Shooting of Dan McGrew*. In 2000, a memorial to the poet was unveiled in the town centre.

Wheelchair access is to the ground floor only, and access to the top of the tower is by steep winding stairs.

HOW TO GET THERE

Take the A78 to Kilwinning. Parking is available either north or south of the Main Street. Trains and buses run from Glasgow, Largs, Ayr or Kilmarnock.

OPENING TIMES

The Abbey ruins and grounds are open at all times. The tower is open June-September, Tues 2-4, Fri & Sat 10.30-12.30 & 2-4, Sunday 2-4. To arrange other times, phone 01294 464174 or 01294 552517.

CHARGES
Free

21
Mother Lodge No. 0
Main Street, Kilwinning
Websites: www.mk0.co.uk
www.thelonius.mit.edu/Masonry/Reports/kilw.html
Website for Kilwinning: www.kilwinning.org

Freemasonry started in earnest at the time of the building of this Abbey in the 12th Century, and it is believed to have its precise origins in Kilwinning. There is, though, a school of thought which claims that freemasonry couldn't have started here, as the masons who built the Abbey came from overseas, and most likely would have brought their guilds and beliefs with them.

The present building, dating from 1883, is known to the worldwide Masonic movement as 'Mother Lodge No. 0'. The reasons for this are slightly complicated, but basically, when the Kilwinning Lodge finally proved its provenance after long arguments about who was first, it was known colloquially as 'Number Nothing'. Eventually, to save renumbering every other Lodge on the planet, the name was formally approved.

The museum contains historical items relating to this and other Lodges, and most interestingly, a Stars and Stripes flag which once was flown over the Capitol building in Washington DC, and which was gifted to the Lodge.

The Kilwinning Lodge was patronised by King James I who was even Grand Master for a while, an honourary title, presumably, as I can't quite picture him wielding a hammer and chisel like ordinary mortals.

It's not unusual to see overseas tourists taking photographs outside. When I visited, it was an official 'Doors Open' day, but I'm told that visitors are always welcome. As one of the members told me, *"People think we're a secret organisation. We're not - we're just an organisation with secrets!"*

HOW TO GET THERE
Directions and parking as for the Abbey. The Lodge is situated right on the Main Street, close to the entrance to the Abbey.

OPENING TIMES
Those in the hood - sorry, the brotherhood - can gain access at any reasonable time, after giving the right signal presumably! Us ordinary punters can ask politely. The museum is usually staffed each afternoon, and I'm sure you'll be welcome.

CHARGES
It's no secret - it's free.
(Free, masons, get it? Oh, please yourself!)

Eglinton Country Park
Irvine KA12 8TA
Tel: 01294 551776   Fax: 01294 556467
Website for Kilwinning: www.kilwinning.org

This beautiful park and castle ruins (see next entry) are set in 1000 acres (400 ha) of lush Ayrshire countryside, designed for leisure and recreation of many kinds. Gifted to the town by businessman R. Clement Wilson who had opened a food processing factory in the old stable block, there are miles of woodland and loch paths, cycle tracks, wildlife habitats, gardens, picnic areas, visitor centre, children's play area, and glassed-over courtyard tearoom.

There's a Ranger service with a wide programme of walks and demonstrations, free wheelchair hire service, even self-catering holiday accommodation in a cottage in the grounds. The visitor centre has an exhibition of the story of the park, which was once one of the most admired estates in Scotland, and the history of the owners, the influential Montgomerie family.

The adjacent Racquets Hall was recently fully restored and houses art exhibitions and other events. Racquets was the predecessor of squash, and apparently was 'invented' by the bored inmates of London's debtors prisons. The Hall is the oldest covered sports hall in Scotland.

Eglinton is most famous for one spectacular, but somewhat disastrous, event. In August 1839, Archibald, the 13th Earl of Eglinton, staged an authentic Medieval Tournament, complete with mounted Knights in full armour and all their servants, feasting, jousting and a Queen of Beauty. The cream of the gentry of the day were its participants. They had been disappointed by the drabness and parsimony of Queen Victoria's Coronation the year before, and it was intended to be a colourful and no-expense-spared party as compensation, indeed, it has been estimated that the event cost the Earl today's equivalent of four MILLION pounds.

The extravagant event attracted an estimated 100,000 spectators from all over the UK and beyond, and it benefitted from the recent completion of the first railway lines in Ayrshire. (It also caused the first fares increase!)

Unfortunately, torrential rain ruined much of the three-day event, creating huge cleaning bills for poor old Archibald, and earning the Tournament an infamous place in history. Spookily, broadly similar conditions dogged the 150th anniversary celebration in 1989. I know - I was there! An excellent book, *The Knight and the Umbrella* by Ian Anstruther, is on sale in the visitor centre, and tells the whole fascinating story of the event.

The magnificent and priceless silver Eglinton Trophy, presented to the 13th Earl by the guests at the Tournament, is on free display in Cunninghame House, headquarters of the local District Council, in nearby Irvine. Ask for directions at Reception. One of the noblemen who contributed to its cost was Prince Louis Napoleon Bonaparte - no, not that one, but a nephew.

23
Eglinton Castle
Eglinton Country Park
Website for Kilwinning: www.kilwinning.org

This is not strictly a castle, but when built as a country house around 1800, it was technically and architecturally described as '*a castellated mansion in the Gothic Revival style*', so there.

The surviving ruin of course, is not the only dwelling to be on this site, since the Montgomerie family lived here since at least the early 1500's. A measure of how 'influential' the family was, lies in the fact that an Earl of Eglinton was one of the authors of the Treaty of Union in 1707, effectively selling Scotland over to English rule. Still, he did all right out of it - he got £200, a fair sum of money in those days.

After his descendants' fortunes declined for reasons other than the expensive Tournament mentioned in the previous entry, the family moved out, the contents of the castle were sold and the roof was removed in 1925.

I live in this area, and I remember my Grandmother telling me she had attended a party in the castle in the early 1900's, my Grandfather being an Estate worker then. Unfortunately, I can't remember any details, apart from her being amazed at the large number of horse-drawn carriages drawing up at the main door, and grand ladies and gentlemen stepping out. Perhaps this was a 'thank you' party for the Estate staff, as it must have been towards the end of the Castle's life.

The Army used the castle for target practice in the last War, and a fine demolition job they made of it too. All that is left now is one tall corner tower and some low walls describing the outline of the basement and ground floors, though as a child, I remember more substantial, but crumbling, remains.

In its time, Eglinton was described as *"unequalled by few places in Scotland, surpassed by none"*. It must have been magnificent indeed, and standing in front of the little that is left, it is not too difficult to imagine it in all its high society splendour. It's a great pity we allowed it to be destroyed.

See also previous entry, 'Eglinton Country Park'.

HOW TO GET THERE (Entries 22 <u>and</u> 23)
Turn off the A78 at Kilwinning and follow the signs. Nearest railway station is Kilwinning. Buses stop near the entrances.
The castle is the focal point of Eglinton Country Park, literally and metaphorically.
You can't miss it.

OPENING TIMES

Park, all year, dawn to dusk.
Visitor Centre, April-October, 10-4.30 daily

CHARGES

Free

24
Glasgow Vennel Museum & Gallery
10 Glasgow Vennel, Irvine KA12 0BD
Tel: 01294 275059
Email: vennal@globalnet.co.uk

The museum is situated in a well-restored 18th Century cobbled street, the main road to Glasgow in the days when Irvine was a major Scottish seaport. The gallery stages changing exhibitions of local, national and international artists, and has a gift shop with pottery, jewellery and other hand crafts.

At the rear is the restored thatched heckling shed museum where Scotland's National Poet, Robert Burns, came in 1781 to learn to dress, or 'heckle', flax and hemp fibres ready for spinning. A video film explains his working life in Irvine. Before then, Burns was a farmer, but not a very successful one, hence the change of profession which he believed would make him both richer, and a more attractive matrimonial prospect.

He set up in partnership with his half-uncle, Alexander Peacock. Burns' wages were £12 per year, plus a share of the profits, but the work was back-breakingly hard, and didn't help Burns' already shaky state of health. His partnership with Peacock was not a happy one. Burns described him as *"a scoundrel of the first order who made money by the mystery of thieving"*, meaning smuggling, a common art in Scotland at that time. Indeed, historians have estimated that in those days, 30% of the population of Irvine was involved in the crime! It is well documented that the unhappy affair came to an abrupt end when the fire broke out, one cold and not entirely sober New Year's Eve. Burns is reputed to have said, *"It wisny me!"*. Well, he probably didn't, but you never know. Conveniently, the blame fell on Mrs Peacock, who no doubt, was as drunk as everyone else, but no-one knows if it was a genuine accident or not.
Afterwards, Burns wrote that he was left, *"like a true poet-without a sixpence!"*.

Nearby is Number 4 Glasgow Vennel, Burns' lodging house, and you can see a recreation of the upstairs room in which he lived. 'Comfortable' and 'cosy' are two words which could not be applied to the small room, and the conditions in which he lived couldn't have helped his health either. The museum has plans to refurbish the room, but these plans depend on grants from the local Council, therefore it will be a long wait.
There is wheelchair access to the gallery and the heckling shed, and toilets. The lodging house is up a steep flight of steps.

HOW TO GET THERE

Irvine is on the A78, north of Ayr. Glasgow Vennel is a narrow street off High Street, heading east from the town centre. The Porthead Tavern, originally the mansion of Provost Charles Hamilton and a friend of Burns, is on the corner.
Trains run from Glasgow and Ayr.

OPENING TIMES

All year, Fri, Sat & Sun, 10-1, 2-5.

CHARGES

Free

24a
The Buchanites Meeting House
Glasgow Vennel, Irvine

As a small aside, you may like to know of another interesting house in Glasgow Vennel. Opposite the Italian restaurant, a restored, private house has its gable end to the street.

This was the house of lawyer Patrick Hunter, known locally by his un-PC name of 'Humphy' Hunter because of his crooked back. A quasi-religious sect took up residence here around 1784, under the leadership of Elspet Buchan, a well-known religious 'zealot', no doubt a euphemism for 'nutcase'. The sect's fanatical but nonconformist activities were famous throughout the district, as Elspet claimed to be able to give immortality to the members by the simple act of breathing on them, and to be able to send them to Heaven without the inconvenience of anyone actually dying.

Being neighbours, the sect attracted the attention of Robert Burns. He claimed to have been "personally acquainted" with most of them. Quite what that means, knowing his reputation with the ladies, and in the light of the following quotation, nobody knows for sure. However, he wrote of them,

"Their tenets are a strange jumble of religious jargon ... she (Elspet) *pretends to give them the Holy Ghost by breathing on them, which she does with postures and practices that are scandalously indecent...*

...they have likewise disposed of all their effects and hold a community of goods, and live nearly an idle life, carrying on a great farce of pretended devotion in barns and woods, where they lodge and lie all together, and hold a community of women, as it is another of their tenets that they can commit no moral sin".

In other words - HIPPIES!

But remember, dear readers, this was the 1780's, not the 1960's, and their behaviour outraged the townspeople (or perhaps they were secretly jealous!). They were not ready for revolutionary ideas of free love and communal property, and were satisfied that the whole group would go to Hell in a Handcart.

Twice, the Buchanites were run out of town by angry mobs, but twice they came back. Finally, the Town Council lost its patience, and formally and forcefully evicted them. When the day arrived, they had to run the gauntlet of yet another jeering crowd, but they left with their heads held high, singing Psalms and declaring they were heading for the New Jerusalem. "No' far enough!", the crowd shouted back, but they only got as far as Kirkudbrightshire in the south west of Scotland, and quite a bit short of their fabled destination.

Elspet Buchan died a few years later, but embarrassingly, it was through natural causes.
"Er, hang on a minute", said her disciples, "I thought we were immortal.......?". Oops.

Disillusioned, the sect broke up, and some of her followers sheepishly returned to Irvine, rejoining the established Church with profound apologies and many promises to behave themselves in future. If there had been such things as tabloid newspapers in those days, they could have sold their story for a small fortune, and we would have known every lurid and scandalous detail.

The Scots novelist John Galt, who was born in Irvine, wrote that he remembered the day of the mass eviction as a young boy. In fact, along with many other children, he merrily joined in the parade! However, his alert mother spotted him and grabbed him by the ear, which probably led to a sore backside as well, but her action saved his future genius for the nation.

HOW TO GET THERE

Directions are as for Chapter 24 'Glasgow Vennel Museum and Gallery'.

Left:
Cross the Bridge of Invention to "The Big Idea", Irvine's £13 million visitor centre and exhibition .

The high-tech centre celebrates 100 years of Nobel Science Prizes.

For full details see chapter 30.

25
Irvine Burns Club & Burgh Museum

'Wellwood', 28 Eglinton Street, Irvine KA12 8AS
Tel: 01294 274551 or 313886
Email: sylvander@irvineburns.ndirect.co.uk
Website: www.irvineburns.ndirect.co.uk

The Irvine club, of which I am a Life Member, is the oldest continuously-meeting Burns Club in the world, being founded by, amongst others, two of the poet's friends in 1826. The museum houses many artefacts, not only of Burns and his time, but also of 600 years of municipal history of the Royal Burgh of Irvine.

It has a fine library of Burnsiana, some relics and personal possessions of the poet, and the original manuscripts of six of his poems. They include *The Twa Dogs, The Holy Fair,* and *The Cotter's Saturday Night,* all of which were the ones used by the printer for Burns' first published works in 1786, the by-now priceless 'Kilmarnock Edition'.

An excellent audio visual display in a separate room recounts the life and times of the poet.

The collection also has 150 years' worth of Holograph letters from famous Honorary Members of Irvine Burns Club, including Dickens, Tennyson, Churchill, Field Marshall Montgomery, Yehudi Menuhin, Garibaldi, Jack Nicklaus, Roosevelt, Douglas Fairbanks Jnr, several Prime Ministers, and many, many famous others.

It is a condition of the offer of Honorary membership that they accept in their own handwriting, hence the term 'holograph' - it's nothing to do with lasers!

HOW TO GET THERE

Irvine is on the A78. Eglinton Street is a northern continuation of High Street. The museum is a red sandstone building, easily identified by the ornamental lamp posts outside. There's limited street parking, otherwise use the public car parks nearby.

OPENING TIMES

Easter-Sept, Mon, Wed, Fri, Sat, 2.30 4.30.
Oct-March, Saturday only, 2.30-4.30.

Pre-booked groups welcome outwith these hours. Contact the Secretary at any of the above addresses.

CHARGES

Free

The Scottish Maritime Museum

Gottries Road, Irvine KA12 8QE
Tel: 01294 278283 Fax: 01294 313211
Email: smm.tildesley.fs.business.co.uk
Website: www.scottishmaritime.museum.org

The museum covers a fairly large area of Irvine's rejuvenated Harbourside, and can be divided into several sections.

There is a collection of vessels which you can see around, moored at pontoons in the harbour, including the Clyde 'puffer' *Spartan,* the lifeboat *St Cybi,* and the *Carola,* 102 years old and the oldest working steam yacht in the UK.

In 1992 the museum acquired what was left of the sailing vessel *Carrick,* the world's oldest colonial clipper, and older than the more famous *Cutty Sark.* At first named 'The City of Adelaide', she took some three thousand First and Second Class emigrants from Scotland to Australia in the second half of the 19th Century.

The museum's plan was to have her fully restored to her original condition, but because of a lack of long-term funds, nearly bankrupting the museum, the work didn't get very far. This was despite her being an 'A' listed vessel, the only vessel in Scotland to be classed as such.

Having this honour should open all sorts of doors, not to mention wallets, you might think. Not so. What it really means is that you can't so much as hammer a nail in without permission being applied for in triplicate, posted in, queried, posted back, lost, found, posted in again, subjected to the closest possible scrutiny if not a public inquiry, lost again, found again, and finally used to plug a leaky roof for six months.

Australia has expressed an interest in having her come 'home' for restoration. So has Sunderland, where she was built in 1864, but they have no money.

At the time of writing, a meeting, chaired by Prince Philip, has agreed that The National Maritime Trust will assume ownership of the vessel, she will revert to her original name, and she will go to the highest bidder.
If not, somebody will have several hundred tons of very historic firewood. It's a great pity that Scotland cares so little about this fascinating and important piece of its own history, but Australia is her only chance of preservation, anywhere.

Nearby, in Montgomery Street, is the Shipyard Worker's Flat, a 'room and kitchen' apartment, restored to the accurate conditions of the 1900's, but mercifully without the damp and the bugs.

Another acquisition is a huge engine shed, known as the Linthouse building, moved brick-by-brick from the Alexander Stephen shipyard in Glasgow.

It formed the heart of a busy Clyde shipbuilder, and, funds permitting, will become THE major part of the museum in years to come.

Restored machines, working engines and other tools will be on show, with video displays, hands-on exhibits, café and changing displays. I've even heard talk of plans to have a full-size cut-away ship that visitors can walk around.
Guided tours are available, and there is a small exhibition area, gift shop and tearoom. There is access for the disabled, except on the vessels, obviously.

HOW TO GET THERE

Irvine is on the A78. Follow the signs to Harbourside, and when you get there, you're there!

The museum complex is only a few hundred yards from the railway station.

OPENING TIMES

All year, 10-5 daily.

CHARGES

Adults & children £,
family ticket £££.

The museum is home to the hulk of the world's oldest colonial clipper "The Carrick" which can be seen in the background.

27
Magnum Leisure Centre & Beach Park
Harbourside, Irvine
Tel: 01294 278381   Fax: 01294 311228
Website: www.themagnum.co.uk

The Magnum is Scotland's largest indoor leisure facility, and is one of the largest in Europe. Its five integrated pools have great water features, with water slides, integrated heated outdoor pool, jacuzzi, hot tub, underwater jets, waterfalls, and Scotland's only white knuckle water flume, the Thunderbowl. I tried the slides once, but only once!

There's also a huge ice rink for skating, curling or ice hockey (but not all at the same time, please!), indoor bowling rinks, squash courts, games hall, a theatre which doubles as a very good cinema, children's soft play areas, fitness suite, sauna, sunbeds, sports shop, bar and café. There is full disabled access with lifts. Scottish Tourist Board Commended.

Beyond and around the Magnum lies the well-laid out Beach Park, site of many noisily successful BBC Radio 1 Roadshows. It's a huge area, reclaimed from 150 acres (60 Ha) of industrial wasteland and undeveloped backshore.

There's a boating pond, jogging track, seasonal funfair, grass maze, wheelchair course, a mini amphitheatre made famous because the band Oasis played there just before they hit the Big Time, picnic areas, and loads of fresh sea breezes, perfect for kite flying.

The beach itself is great when it's tidy, with its magnificent curve south towards Troon and Ayr, but as far as swimming goes, remember what I said in the Introduction about pollution. You'll get a panoramic view of the whole bay and the island of Arran.

HOW TO GET THERE

Irvine is on the A78.
Follow the signs for Harbourside. The Magnum is a big square building near the beach, with 'MAGNUM' painted on the side in large, friendly letters.

Trains run from Glasgow and Ayr, then it's a 10 min. walk from the station.
Local buses run from the town.

OPENING TIMES

Swimming:
Mon & Fri 9-9. Tues-Thurs 10-9,
Sat & Sun 9-5.
Skating:
Mon-Fri 10-4, late sessions Mon & Fri 7-10.
Sat 12.15-4.30. Sun 11.15-4.30.
Hours outwith peak summer period may vary.

CHARGES

Swimming - ££ adults, £ children. Flume extra.
Concessions and family tickets available.
Skating - £ adults. £ juniors. Skate hire £.
Friday night skating disco ££.
Prices for other activities variable. Phone for details.

28
Harbour Arts Centre
Harbour Street, Irvine KA12 8PZ
Tel: 01294 274059   Fax: 01294 217419
Email:admin@nachac.prestel.co.uk
Website:www.harbourarts.org.uk

Like Members of Parliament, I must declare another interest here, and state that I've been a member since 1970, but I'll try to stay objective!

The building was originally a seaman's mission hall at the end of the 19th Century. During the last World War, it was designated as an emergency mortuary, although we don't believe it was actually used as such. However, this has led to stories about it being haunted by what we've come to call The Old Captain. Nothing weird has happened to me, but I could tell you some odd tales. . . . .

It has also been used as a Scout 'hut' and part of it (the bar) was even a private residence for a time! After service as a small knitwear factory, it became the Harbour Arts Centre in 1966. In the early 70's, the Centre was extended and refurbished, partly by a volunteer workforce, including me, and I still bear the scars! It also founded and was the first base of Borderline, one of Scotland's best-known touring theatre companies, but they now operate from Ayr.

Normally, there is a busy programme, run on a shoestring budget by a few volunteers and even fewer staff, and funded almost entirely by the District Council. There is an intimate 96-seat theatre where some of the best small-scale touring companies, solo artistes and amateur groups appear, a gallery with new exhibitions every month, day and evening art classes, children's art and drama courses, local bands on Friday evenings, 'Unplugged' acoustic sessions on Sunday afternoons, amateur drama classes for all ages and abilities, and other workshop and seasonal activities. The annual three-week Art Summer School is almost always oversubscribed by patrons from far and wide. Disabled access is available for all performances and classes.

Great plans for more expansion are afoot, pending a successful application for Lottery funding, but, oh boy, the wheels grind slowly........

HOW TO GET THERE

If you've found the Magnum, you've found the Centre, as it's in front of it in Harbour Street, between the Marina Inn and the Ship Inn on Irvine's Harbourside.

OPENING TIMES

Gallery Tues, Wed, Thurs, Sat, 10-4, all year.
Closed end Dec-mid Jan.
Bar open on Friday nights, Saturday show nights and Sunday afternoons.

CHARGES

Gallery and bar events free.
Other classes and performances variable, typically around ££ or £££ for theatre events.
Concessions available.

Pilot House, Irvine Harbour

Worth a mention, if only because it is unique in the world.

Built in 1906, this square white four-storey tower had an automatic tide-signalling device on the roof, invented by Martin Boyd, harbour master of the day, but which is now out of use. It acted like a ballcock in a toilet cistern, with large spheres on the roof rising and falling by a system of floats on the water, wires and pulleys, informing approaching vessels of the state of the tide in the harbour. The more balls visible, the higher the tide.

A similar, but different, system worked at night, when coloured screens were raised or lowered in the lighted windows of the tower, in place of the spheres.
It's only viewable from the outside, but as I said, it is unique and therefore, special. If you're going down to the beach, which is as far as you can go in Harbour Street, it's at the harbour mouth. If you're into maritime history, take the trip.

HOW TO GET THERE

Go all the way down Harbour Street, past all the pubs, leisure centres and arts centres you can find. Just before the road comes to a dead end along the old wharf, turn left, then right, and go past the big car parks.
The road comes to a roundabout, and the Pilot House is right in front of you. Park near here and enjoy the beach and the view. On stormy days, it's a popular place to go and look at the waves.

Left:
The Pilot House, once the home of a unique maritime signalling system. In the background "The Big Idea" and its bridge can be seen.

30
The Big Idea
Harbourside, Irvine KA12 8XX
Tel: 087088 404030
Email: net@bigidea.org.uk
Website: www.bigidea.org.uk

At Irvine's Harbourside, across the river from the beach car parks, is the sandy Ardeer peninsula. The scientist and inventor Alfred Nobel began dynamite production here in 1875, and the whole area is now owned by I.C.I. On a site closest to the river mouth is The Big Idea. But note that it is not a museum. It is an Inventor Centre. It is totally unique, being the only permanent visitor attraction in the world dedicated solely to inventions. This is one of the newest attractions in Ayrshire, opening at Easter 2000.

The Big Idea celebrates 100 years of Nobel Science Prizes and 1000 years of inventions. The £13m glass-fronted building has been built to resemble a sand dune, and its roof is covered in grass and heather. (Local wags have already suggested that sheep should be imported to keep the grass trimmed!) Inside are major exhibits covering communications, energy, mechanisms, materials, explosives, and details of many of Nobel's inventions, and they're all 'hands on'. Upon entry, you can choose an inventions kit, and can use the parts to build your own electrical or mechanical device, test it, and take it home. Also, you receive an 'I-Button', which activates each exhibit for you, and allows you free access in and out of the exhibits to visit the restaurant or shop.

The highlight for me and my two grandsons though, was the pink-knuckle ride, The History of Explosions. It's like a small IMAX-type cinema, and you and a couple of dozen others are taken on a 'ride' through the Millennia, from The Big Bang, to the invention of gunpowder and nuclear fission, and ending with space flight. Throughout the ride, the floor bucks and jolts, and lights, sounds and smoke add to the thrill. Needless to say, it may not be suitable for toddlers, pregnant women, anyone with neck or back trouble or, as they say, those of a nervous disposition. But it's not a Roller Coaster, so it's not so much scary, as exciting.

The Ardeer site has a long history in this area, and at its peak, it employed more than 18,000 people. Generations of many local families spent their entire working lives here, and one section tells some of their stories through a giant, interactive "family tree".
There is a restaurant and a large shop filled with technological items and toys of all types, and full disabled access.

HOW TO GET THERE

Follow the signs from the town centre and main roads surrounding the town.

Go right down Harbour Street to the large car park.

OPENING TIMES

10-6 daily, all year.

CHARGES

(Charges, explosives - get it? Oh, please yourself.)
Free access to restaurant and shop.
Adults ££££, concessions £££,
family tickets available.

31
Dundonald Castle
4 Winehouse Yett, Dundonald KA2 9HD
Tel: 01563 851489
Website: www.royaldundonaldcastle.co.uk

Extensive archeological excavation has revealed that this hilltop site was occupied before 2000BC. Interesting enough, you might think, but hang on, it gets better. This castle is not generally well known, being neglected by successive tourist and government authorities. Recently, constant pressure from the Friends of Dundonald Castle finally paid off in a multi-million pound restoration. Historically, it's important because of its Royal connections, it's reckoned to be third in order of importance after Edinburgh and Stirling castles. Pay attention now, this is the history bit . . . .

It was founded around 1150 by Walter the Steward, progenitor of the Stewart dynasty of seven Scottish Kings, one Queen (Mary Queen of Scots), and seven British monarchs. Then, it was a fairly simple earthwork and timber affair. Around 1300, it was completely rebuilt in stone by Alexander Stewart, and was very grand, having battlements, towers, turrets and men in tights. Following partial demolition after occupation by English troops, the castle was rebuilt again in 1371 by Robert II, grandson of The Bruce, to celebrate his own succession to the throne, and it became his favourite residence. It passed in to the hands of the Wallaces (yes, the "Braveheart" Wallaces) in 1526.

On the first floor, there was a large feasting hall, used for, well, large feasts. There were huge vaults underneath, used for storing the things that were eaten at the large feasts. Feasts were an important part of Courtly life. Hospitality shown by the King was seen as a display of power, wealth and gracious generosity, and it is said that feasts required as much physical endurance as any Tournament. These were times when table manners weren't considered terribly important. Basically, if you were a visiting knight, you were expected to eat, drink and behave outrageously until you threw up and fell over, a bit like New Year celebrations nowadays, only without the guilt. To service these consequences, many latrines were thoughtfully built into the fabric of the walls! Robert II died here in 1390, as did his son Robert III in 1406, probably of too much feasting if you ask me.

The Visitor Centre has interpretive displays and models of the various styles of castle on the site, guides, gifts and souvenirs, and a tearoom for small feasting. Helpful and friendly guides will explain the features of the castle and the various aspects of castle life. As it sits on top of a hill, disabled access is to the visitor centre only, otherwise, it's a pretty steep climb up to the castle.

HOW TO GET THERE

The village of Dundonald is on the A759 Troon to Kilmarnock road, 12 miles (19 km) north of Ayr and 5 miles (8 km) west of Kilmarnock. Take the Dundonald turnoff from the A71 Irvine to Kilmarnock road, or the signposted turnoff from the A77 Glasgow to Ayr route. It stands on a hill and is quite a landmark, so you can't miss it.

OPENING TIMES

Visitor Centre, Apr-Sept 10-5 daily. Last ticket sold at 3.30. Castle exterior free to view at all times.

CHARGES

Adults £.
Concessions for children.

32
Dick Institute
Elmbank Avenue, Kilmarnock KA1 3BU
Tel: 01563 554343

'The Dick', as it's known locally, was a gift to the town in 1901 from James Dick, a local boy who had made good. James had an upholstery business in Glasgow, but when *gutta-percha*, a natural latex rubber, came on the market in quantity, he exploited its potential for making long-lasting shoe soles, and his fortune was secured. Even today, some Scots refer to waterproof footwear as "gutties". (Honest!)

As well as the public library, the building stages fascinating and sometimes unique temporary exhibitions, like the recent biggest exhibition of Burns artefacts ever presented.

It also has a fine museum with a notable collection of geological, archaeological, and natural history exhibits. Kids will particularly enjoy the collection of dead creepy-crawlies, moths and other bugs!

It also houses what is amongst Ayrshire's best genealogical research facilities, so if your folks came from around these here parts, and you're trying to trace them, try here.

The art gallery has works by Turner, Constable, and other notable ranks, and hosts important touring exhibitions. There's a restaurant and shop and full disabled access.

HOW TO GET THERE

Kilmarnock is on the A77 Glasgow to Ayr road, or take the A71 from Irvine.
From the town centre Ring Road which, like me, you'll probably go round a couple of times, take the B7073 towards Hurlford and Galston.
The Dick is on the right, at the junction of London Road and Elmbank Avenue.
Trains run to Kilmarnock from Glasgow and Ayr.

OPENING TIMES

Museum:
Summer
10-8 Mon, Tues, Thurs, Fri.
10-5 Wed & Sat.
Winter
10-5 Mon-Sat.
Art Gallery:
All year, same as museum summer hours.

CHARGES

Free

Loudoun Castle Family Theme Park
Galston KA4 8PE
Tel: 01563 822296 Fax: 01563 822408
Email: Castle@btinternet.com
Website:www.loudouncastle.co.uk (Highly recommended!)

This is the site of Scotland's largest Theme Park, opened in 1995 in 500 acres of parkland. Geared for the whole family, there's the huge funfair and white knuckle rides of course, and also a children's farm, putting greens, museum, pony rides and countryside walks.

Rory's Farmyard has llamas, emus, farm animals and the Park's own breed of Highland Cattle, the hairy brown ones with big horns and dripping noses (see picture below).

The funfair has the biggest Carousel in the UK, dodgems, roundabouts, log flume, ghost train, go karts, rollercoasters, and lots of rides for the little ones too. New for the 21st Century is the 140 ft (45m) Drop Zone, from the top of which you are violently and abruptly dropped earthwards at a force of 2 G's! I'll pass on that one, thank you.

Entertainment at Loudoun Castle is not a new idea, though. In 1714, the Third Earl of Loudoun drew up plans for a *'menagery'* and a *'Howse of entertaynmente'*, and yes, they've heard all the jokes about it taking them 281 years to get started! The estate is the ancestral home of the Campbells of Loudoun, who can trace their family tree back as far as the 11th Century King David I. The present ruin, destroyed by fire in 1941, was known as the 'Windsor of Scotland', and dates from 1804.

The estate also has family associations with - guess who - William Wallace. One of his swords was a treasured heirloom until 1930, when it was removed to the Wallace Monument in Stirling.

The house had its ghosts, of course. There's the inevitable Grey Lady, who latterly, was so well-known, she was treated almost as one of the family.

There's also the equally inevitable Phantom Piper, but perhaps most interestingly, the Benevolent Monk, who pops up here and there in the grounds and whispers *"Pax Vobiscum"* (Peace be with you) in the ear of an unsuspecting passer-by!

The Castle has an extremely important part in Scotland's history. Tradition states that the terms and conditions of The Treaty of Union of 1707 were thrashed out at Loudoun. The Treaty united Scotland with England and signalled the end of Scotland as a separate nation. Of course, some Scottish nobles only signed the treaty in return for money, land and power. (See also entry, 'Eglinton Castle')

These acts are derided in a Robert Burns song, *Parcel O' Rogues'*, which lambasted the nobles for selling Scotland in the line, "We're bought and sold for English gold, such a parcel o' rogues in a nation". Oh well.

HOW TO GET THERE

Take the A71 east from Kilmarnock for about 5 miles (8 km).

At Galston, turn left onto the A719 (signposted to Moscow!), and it's about half a mile on the right.

OPENING TIMES

Easter school holidays, seven days.
End April-end September 10-5 seven days. Some weekends in April, May and September, and October school holidays. Phone first for details.

CHARGES

One payment gets you entry to everything, and as many goes as you want.
Children's prices depend on their size/age.
Adults & tall/older children - £££££,
smaller/younger children - ££££
Children under 90 cm (35 ins) - free.
Concessions & non-riders - ££££
If you spend the whole day here, great value family tickets are available.

34
Dean Castle Country Park
Dean Road. Kilmarnock KA3 1XB
Tel: 01563 522702
Fax: 01563 572552

Dean Castle is a gem. It's a fantastic place, and I don't understand why it's not much more famous. Kids will love it, because there's real armour, real swords, and loads of gory (and some disgusting) stories about the place. And it's FREE!

I accord it high praise, and I promise you'll be impressed. Unlike a lot of castles, which are merely country houses with pretensions, this is a 'proper' castle, with dungeons and battlements and stuff like that. If you stand in the courtyard, you'll think you're on a Hollywood film set!

These lands were owned by the Boyd family, whose influence went from fighting the Vikings at the Battle of Largs in 1263 (see chapter 11 'Pencil Monument') to Culloden in 1746. Robert Boyd had been gifted the land by Robert the Bruce as a reward for his loyalty in fighting for William Wallace at the Battle of Bannockburn.

The original sturdy keep with its three metre-thick walls was built around 1350, and is now completely restored, as is the adjoining Palace of a later date.
The castle reinforces its macho image with a hair-raising display of genuine Medieval armour and weapons, including a set of battle armour for a knight's horse. There is also a surprisingly interesting set of beautiful Flemish 15th and 16th Century tapestries, and an extremely important collection of early musical instruments such as guitars, lutes and keyboards. This is one of the finest collections of these rare, delicate and beautiful objects to be seen anywhere on the planet, and shouldn't be missed, particularly if you're a musician of any type. Look out for the gold Serpent. . . . . .

There's also a small collection of Burns artefacts, including a manuscript of 'Tam O'Shanter'. The friendly guides have all sorts of stories about the castle, will show you the Lord of the Castle's toilet, will tell you about the severed head in the box, and will explain precisely just how disgusting was the dungeon. There's a guide book in comic form for youngsters, and they can fill in the answers as the tour progresses.

The 200-acre Country Park hosts a variety of activities. There's the Visitor Centre, with information about the wildlife to be seen on the miles of the Park's woodland walks. The Rare Breeds centre has cuddly animals and colourful birds.

In the Children's Corner, youngsters can feed the birds, goats, sheep and ponies. The Rangers offer other activities like Fungus Hunts and Ghost Walks. After all that, you can visit the shop or the tearoom at the Visitor Centre.

In good weather, you can easily spend the whole day here. Wheelchair access is to the Park, Visitor Centre, Castle courtyard, shop and medieval kitchen.
Note - there are steep stairways inside the castle.

Visitors can easily spend a day exploring Dean Castle (above) and its 200 acre Country Park.

OPENING TIMES

Easter-October,
tours of castle 12-5 daily.
Nov-March 12-4
weekends only.
Visitor Centre open daily,
11-5 Summer, 11-4 Winter.
Country Park and
Children's Corner
dawn till dusk all year.
Rare Breeds Centre daily,
1-5 Summer, 1-4 Winter.
Closed Xmas and New Year.

HOW TO GET THERE

Follow the brown signs from the A77 Glasgow to Ayr road. If you're in the town and get lost on the one-way system, follow the *'A77 Glasgow'* signs. Trains run to Kilmarnock from Glasgow and Ayr, then it's a 20 minute walk to the park.

CHARGES

It's all free, and because there's so much to see and do, it's easily the best value visitor attraction you'll come across.

Top:
The Abbey Tower stands next to the ruins of floodlit Kilwinning Abbey.
See chapter 20 for details.

Historic Eglinton Castle in its heyday (top) and, below, all that remains of the castle today.
See chapters 22 and 23 for details.

Above: You can choose from many leisure activities at Irvine Harbourside. See chapters 26-30 for more details.
Below: The region has its share of unspoilt villages and hamlets. This one—Corrie on the Isle of Arran—sits next to the sea.

Above: The Pencil Monument at Largs commemorates the Battle of Largs in 1263. (See chapter 11).
Below: Dundonald Castle (see chapter 31) has many Royal connections.

Ayr, is of course, the county town of Ayrshire and is central for most of the attractions featured in this book.

Eglinton Country Park - *a great day out for all the family*

Eglinton Country Park, created around the ruins and estate policies of Eglinton Castle, includes formal gardens, woodland, rivers, loch and Visitor Centre. A ranger service is available to give guided walks and provide an interpretive service.

NORTH AYRSHIRE
COUNCIL

- Visitor Centre
- Gift Shop
- Car/coach park
- Café/Tearoom
- Ranger Service
- Picnic areas
- Cycling
- Angling
- Horse riding
- Walks/trails
- Children's play areas

Admission Free

Country Park open all year. Visitor Centre open April—October.

The Visitor Centre
Eglinton Country Park, Irvine KA12 8TA
Tel: 01294 551776 Fax 01294 556467
E-mail: georgeclark@naceglintonpk.prestel.co.uk

Discover the heritage of North Ayrshire

NORTH AYRSHIRE MUSEUM
Manse Street
Saltcoats, KA21 5AA
01294 464174

Enjoy the rich social history of North Ayrshire from prehistoric times to the present day.

VENNEL GALLERY
10 Glasgow Vennel,
Irvine, KA12 0BD.
01294 275059.

Robert Burns once lived and worked here. It is now home to contemporary art and crafts.

KILWINNING ABBEY TOWER
Main Street
Kilwinning
01294 464174

Find out all about Kilwinning and enjoy marvellous views across Ayrshire.

MUSEUM OF THE CUMBRAES
Garrison Grounds
Millport, KA28 0DG
01475 531191

No trip doon the watter is complete without a visit to this fascinating wee museum.

NORTH AYRSHIRE
COUNCIL

Kid'z Play
The Esplanade, Prestwick KA9 1QG
Tel: 01292 475215
Website: www.kidz-play.co.uk

Pirate Pete's
The Pavilion, The Esplanade, Low Green, Ayr KA7 1DT
Tel: 01292 265300   Fax: 01292 264006
Email: info@piratepetes.co.uk
Website: www.piratepetes.co.uk

I've included these two on the sam3 pages, as both have similar facilities, but with different themes. Both are safe indoor play areas for the under 12's, perfect for wet days. They are ideal places for kids that have had enough of castles or country parks or visitor centres. Stick them in here, let them run riot for a couple of hours, and they'll definitely sleep that night!

KIDZ PLAY:

At Kid'z Play, under 5's can play in the Jungle Village, a toddler-size town with Jungle Kitchen, Swamp Ball Pool, and the crazily-named Bongo Bouncer, where presumably one can Bounce one's Bongoes 'til one's Bushed.

5 to 12 year-olds will have fun in the Jungle Adventure, the climbing frame to end all climbing frames. There are three levels of swings, slides and obstacles, all safely padded, with names like the Wavy Slide, the Zig Zag Maze, the Canyon Causeway, the Spooky Cave, or the Indiana Jones Giant Ball Run.

Parents can retire to the Bananas Café to relax with snacks or meals, whilst still keeping an eye on the youngsters. Note that, as safety is one of their strong points, only adults who are with paying children are permitted inside. Baby changing facility. Disabled access. Tourist Board Commended.

PIRATE PETE'S:

At Pirate Pete's, there are play areas to suit all ages up to 12. Kids can clamber in an out of four levels of all kinds of games and adventure. For Mini Mutineers up to 5 years old, there are slides, a ball pool lagoon, a spook room and lots more.

If you're over 5, you're a Mighty Marauder, and you can walk the plank, after you've scaled the nets, gone down the slides, and done all the other stuff that pirates do.

The restaurant has a large menu, sure to satisfy the most demanding palate. Yearly membership available.
At both places, trained staff are on hand to make sure the equipment isn't abused, and that everyone's enjoying themselves, but you must remember that they are not child

minders, so you must make sure that a responsible adult is with your child at all times. They are popular places for birthday party treats, and they'll do you a good deal with exclusive play time, juice, ice cream, freebies, cake, etc.

Phone for details of this service.

HOW TO GET THERE

PIRATE PETE'S:

From Ayr town centre, head towards the sea, where you'll find the esplanade. The Low Green is a large open grassy area at the esplanade. The Pavilion is a large white building with a tower in each corner, adjacent to the County Buildings. It's a 2 minute walk from the main bus station or 5 minutes from the railway station.

KIDZ PLAY:

From Ayr or Prestwick Airport direction, head for Prestwick town centre.
At The Cross, turn towards the railway station down Station Road, then into Links Road.
At the sea front, turn right, and you're there. Trains go from Ayr and Glasgow to Prestwick Town, then it's only a five minute walk.

OPENING TIMES

PIRATE PETE'S:

9.30-7 Sun-Thurs.
9.30-7.30 Fri-Sat

CHARGES

(Price per 2 hour session)
Weekdays - ££,   Weekends - £££,
Holidays - £££,   Last hour - £.
Adults & babes-in-arms free.
Party prices - phone for details.

KIDZ PLAY:

Sun-Thurs 9.30-7,
Fri-Sun 9.30- 7.30,
except Xmas &
New Year's Day.

CHARGES

Children ££ per two hour session
(applicable at peak times)
Adults and babies free.

36
Craigie Horticultural & Visitor Centre
Craigie Estate, Ayr KA8 0SS
(Also the address for the **Ayrshire Archives Centre**)
Tel. 01292 263275

The Centre is owned and operated by South Ayrshire Council. Educational courses are available in a huge range of gardening topics, including garden design, greenhouses, lawns, roses, Alpines, trees, vegetables, ponds, aquatic plants and herbaceous borders, but casual visitors are its daily bread and butter. It's popular with school parties, who get hands-on teaching about plants and all aspects of horticulture.

The Floral Hall has displays of giant cacti and other tender plants from The Americas, Australia, and the Mediterranean. The Tropical Glasshouse has orchids and other exotic rainforest plants (a nice place to go in winter!). It also has a fish pond where beautiful Koi carp swim lazily. The Demonstration Glasshouse and shop are the first places you should head for if you're after practical experience and demonstrations.

The Information Centre will give free advice on all your gardening problems, and after being inspired, the sales area will satisfy your new-found enthusiasm with a wide range of houseplants, floral art and gardening supplies. When you're exhausted with all that, relax in the tearoom with its delicious home baking and snacks.

The Centre is in the attractive and peaceful wooded grounds of Craigie Estate, and is within easy walking distance from the railway station and town centre.

Craigie Estate is also home to **Ayrshire Archives Centre**. It is the base for Ayrshire's local government and historic records, some dating back to the 14th Century, and it also holds some private collections of family, parish and business records.

It can be used by historians and casual visitors. They also operate an enquiry service, for which there is a charge.

For further information, contact the centre on 01292 287584, (Fax 01292 284918). Their email address is archives@south-ayrshire.gov.uk

HOW TO GET THERE

From the town centre or the station, head for the racecourse.

The gates to the estate are on the right, just past the roundabout where the fire station and the Civic Theatre are situated. It's a ten-minute walk from the railway station.

OPENING TIMES

Horticultural Centre all year,
10-5 daily.
Ayrshire Archives
Tues-Thurs 10-1, 2-4.30

CHARGES

Free

37
Haven Holiday Park
Craig Tara Holiday Park, Ayr KA7 4LB.
Tel. 01292 265141.
Website: www.haven-holidays.co.uk

There are 55 Haven Holiday Parks in the UK, designed for short or long-term breaks, and stretching from Inverness to Land's End. One is in Ayrshire.

This one, formerly Butlin's Wonderwest World is now called Craig Tara, nothing to do with Gone With The Wind, and a name that I suspect has been invented, but no harm to it.

Accommodation is in apartments or caravans sleeping up to eight, but there are sites for touring caravans or motor homes.

If you think you know about these kinds of parks from the TV series 'Hi De Hi', you'll be doing them an injustice, as things have moved on a lot from those times. True, everything is laid on for you if you wish, but Craig Tara can also be used as a base for travelling around the area. The site has indoor pools and other amusements and sports facilities, bars and restaurants, and entertainment venues. In other words, there is loads for kids and adults to do, whatever the weather.

It is termed an All-Action Park, meaning a large park with top facilities, and it's right on the coast with its own beach. £14 million is being spent to upgrade and modernise the entertainment facilities and accommodation, and there's plenty to do - the Splash Zone indoor fun pool and flumes, Fun Palace, adventure playground, all-weather sports pitch, Crystal Quay entertainment complex, go karts, Circus Crazy, family summer shows, mini golf, and loads more.

For youngsters, it has the Rompers play area and the Tiger Club, while 10's to young teens have the T-CO Club. There are loads of restaurants and fast food places, including a branch of Harry Ramsden's Fish and Chips!

Note: No day visitors.

HOW TO GET THERE

Craig Tara is on the A719 coast road, just south of Ayr.

OPENING TIMES

Beginning of April to end of October.

CHARGES

Prices vary enormously, depending on accommodation and season.
Any good travel agent should have full details and brochures.

38
Heads of Ayr Farm Park
Dunure Road, Ayr KA7 4HR
Tel/Fax: 01292 441210
Email: info@headsofayrpark.co.uk
Website: www.headsofayrpark.co.uk

Set in 125 acres (50ha), with beautiful views over the Firth of Clyde, this is more like an open zoo. There are loads of great animals here, about fifty in all - llamas, pigs, horses, a turkey called Xmas, wallabies, alpacas, African cattle, Duke the buffalo, a mouse farmyard, rats, rabbits, peacocks, ducks, goats, owls, chipmunks, guinea pigs, Monty the python, frogs, snakes, iguanas, a rhea called Chris (Chris Rea - get it?), and you can feed many of them, but not to each other, please!

Also here are buggy rides, childrens' quad bikes, summer grass sledging, pony rides, aerial runway, giant slides, indoor play areas, trampolines, climbing wall, straw play shed, picnic areas, gift shop, explanatory displays and mercifully, a heated Barn Café.

The friendly staff will answer all your questions, and if you time your visit right, there'll be lambs or Easter chicks and bunnies. It brings a tear to the eye just writing about

it, but the younger kids will love it.

Lots of things are under cover, so you don't need perfect weather.

You should hope though, that Duke the Buffalo isn't indoors in warm weather, as these beasts tend not to bother too much about personal hygiene!

Disabled access.

HOW TO GET THERE

The farm park is 4 miles (6.4 km) south of Ayr on the A719, heading for Culzean Castle.
Nearest railway station is Ayr, then take the bus from the town centre.

OPENING TIMES

Easter-end Oct, 10-5 daily.
(Last admission 4pm)

CHARGES

Adults and concessions £££
Families of up to 5, max 2 adults £££££
Under 2's free

39
Dunure Castle, The Electric Brae & Croy Shore

On the way to Culzean Castle (see chapter 41) by car, you will come to the junction of the road to the small village of Dunure, clinging to the coast. **Dunure Castle**, custom built to fit the large rock it stands on, was latterly much larger than the existing ruin, and is remembered for a few infamous reasons. In 1570, Gilbert Kennedy the 4th Earl of Cassillis, roasted Alan Stewart, the Commendator of nearby Crossraguel Abbey (see separate entry) over an open fire in the castle's Black Vault, and what a perfect name for a torture chamber that is! The torture was effective, of course, and Stewart signed over the Abbey lands. He was rescued by the Earl's bitter enemies, the Bargany Kennedys, and the Earl was ordered to pay compensation, but he refused, and from that time on, the two branches of the Kennedys appeared not to get on much with each other, or indeed anyone else.

The other incident was in 1973, when the members of the old Ayr County Council debated hotly as to what was to happen to the ruined tower. Some argued that it was of historical interest, and should be maintained as an interesting example of local heritage, while others argued that it was a loathsome symbol of a cruel and degrading feudal system, and should be bulldozed forthwith.

It survived. Ayr County Council didn't.

Speaking of ruins, Mary Queen of Scots stayed three nights here, and complained about a stiff neck due to the drafts. (Not as stiff as her neck later became, though!) Some cynics would ask, "Where didn't she stay?", as she got about a bit, but apparently she was here, so there. There's a picnic area with plenty parking. In recent years, there have been excavations and renovation work done to parts of the ruin, so it is again open to public view, with explanatory boards.

A little south of Dunure, you will come across signs for what is known as **The Electric Brae** (a "brae" is a hill). This is a fairly unique optical illusion, and is nothing to do with any kind of electricity - the road goes gently downhill, but because of the slope of the landscape and the general geographic layout, it appears as if your car is freewheeling UPhill! (or maybe it's the other way round......) Try it for yourself by switching the engine off and releasing the handbrake, but watch out for other road users! There is actually a 17ft difference between one end of the road and the other, and try as you might, your car just refuses to roll down the hill (or maybe it's the other way round......).

Next, you will see signs for **Croy Shore**, and you should make a small detour. The narrow road winds carefully down the hill, passing a caravan site until it gets to the beach, where there's another caravan site. Take your car onto the beach and you'll be rewarded with a spectacular sweeping curve of sand, backed by rugged cliffs, where Culzean Castle (see next entry) can be seen. When the wind's in the right direction, impressive waves come crashing in on the shore. It's a great site for a picnic on the beach and memorable photographs, and is a popular place on a sunny day.

HOW TO GET THERE

Take the A719, south of Ayr, and follow the signposts.

Culzean Castle and Country Park
Maybole KA19 8LE
Tel: 01655 884455   Fax: 01655 884503
For Ranger service & Country Park info, phone 01655 884522
Email: culzean@nts.org.uk
Website: www.culzeancastle.net

Culzean (pronounced "Kull-ain") is undoubtedly the jewel in Ayrshire's crown, if you'll pardon the cliché. By any system of measurement, it is one of the most spectacular, attractive and romantic stately homes you're likely to see in Scotland, and thoroughly deserves its Scottish Tourist Board Highly Commended badge. The Shell Book of Country Parks describes it as the most magnificent Country Park in Britain, and it won a Tourism Oscar in 1990 for being the best tourist attraction in Scotland. Quite simply, everything about it is stunning, not least the castle's setting, high on a cliff overlooking the Firth of Clyde with panoramic views to Arran, the Mull of Kintyre, and even Ireland in the distance. Should you visit Ayrshire and not go here, well frankly, you need your head examined. Thankfully, it's not a theme park, it's for relaxing in.

The whole 563 acres (227 ha) was donated to the National Trust for Scotland just after the last war by the Kennedys, a very old family whose real power started in the 15th Century with James Kennedy's marriage to Robert the Bruce's granddaughter. The castle was designed by the world famous Scottish architect Robert Adam in 1777 in the fashionable Neo-Gothic style, and was built around an existing ancient tower house. It has been carefully and fairly completely restored to its original condition, including incidentally, the gateway at the Castle's entrance, which was designed to look like a ruined gatehouse. Built as a country retreat for the 10th Earl of Cassillis so he could show off his wealth to his friends, the interior's design features and plasterwork fittings are the height of Georgian elegance and good taste, and are probably unsurpassed in Scotland. The unique Oval Staircase, built to fill an interior courtyard, and the Circular Saloon, are without compare, and must be seen to be fully appreciated. As you enter through the main door, the walls of the Reception Hall are covered, and I mean COVERED, in an intricate, dense display of hundreds of pistols, swords, daggers and lances. I would love to report that they were the Kennedy family arsenal, but according to the guide, they are Army Surplus, bought as a job lot from the Tower of London!

Inside also, are apartments which belonged to the late U.S. President Dwight D. Eisenhower, a gift from a grateful Scots nation. In Culzean's own 'Oval Office' there are panels, photographs and videos explaining his contribution to WWII along with some of his possessions. The apartments are available for rent, at £300 per night!

The castle is haunted, naturally. There's said to be a phantom piper who plays at times of trouble or change, and there's also the ghost of a young lady. Some say she's the spectre of a mistreated maid, others that she must be nobility, as she appears to be dressed in a ballgown. She was last seen in 1972, but there may have been a recent reappearance. In January 2002, a film crew from a UK satellite TV station visited the castle to shoot material for a programme about haunted buildings. On checking the footage they'd shot at night, they saw mysterious, drifting patches of light at various places around the castle.

The Visitor Centre, itself the winner of several architecture awards, is housed in the nearby and beautifully restored Home Farm buildings. There is an audio-visual theatre, an exhibition of the story of Culzean and of those who lived there, an excellent restaurant, and two National Trust shops. The Park's Rangers are based here too, and they will be happy to explain how they work to conserve the Park's flora and fauna.

In the Country Park are formal and informal gardens, newly-restored Victorian vinery, deer park, aviary, Adventure Playground, Swan Pond, Gas House exhibition, restored Pagoda, Camellia House and Orangery, greenhouses, miles of peaceful woodland and shoreline walks, and picnic areas. In Spring and early Summer the colours of the masses of daffodils and bluebells are blinding.

There are loads of events throughout the year at Culzean - illustrated talks, guided walks, concerts, craft fairs, battle re-enactments, performances of all types, children's events, Classic Car rallies, equestrian events, dog events, even Victorian Christmas events - the list is just about endless, and there is a separate booklet detailing them. During the season, there is something extra to see or do every few days or so.

Foreign language information sheets are available in Dutch, French, German, Italian, Spanish, and Japanese. A Braille guidebook is also available. There is full disabled access and a lift in the castle, and an induction loop system for the hard of hearing in the Visitor Centre auditorium. Wheelchairs and battery cars are available, but book in advance. If you're moving on to "do" any of the 100 or so other National Trust properties in Scotland - for instance, Brodick Castle on Arran (see later) - you can join the Trust here. It'll save you a fortune in the long run.

No disrespect to all the other visitor attractions, but if you've only time to spend one day in Ayrshire, spend it here, and make it the whole day.

HOW TO GET THERE

Culzean is about 12 miles (19 km) south of Ayr on the A719 coastal road, and is well signposted.

The nearest railway station is Maybole, or buses run from Ayr.

OPENING TIMES

Castle & Visitor Centre, Apr 1 (or Good Friday if earlier) to Oct 31, 11-5.30 daily.

Country Park, 9.30-sunset daily, all year.
Castle also open weekends in March, Nov & Dec, guided tours, 12-2.30.

Visitor Centre restaurant also open weekends Jan, Feb, March, Nov & Dec

CHARGES

Park & Castle: ££££, concessions £££, family tickets available.
Park only: £££, conc. ££, family tickets available.
Additional charge for Castle if you change your mind, but it works out the same.
National Trust members free.

If you have only one day to spend in Ayrshire, then spend it at Culzean Castle.
Sitting in its cliff top position, the castle, designed by Robert Adam in 1777, has something for everyone.
For full details, see chapter 40.

41
The Dunaskin Experience
Dalmellington Road, Waterside, Ayrshire KA6 7JF
Tel: 01292 531144
Email: dunaskin@btconnect.com
Website: home.btconnect.com/Dunaskin

Ayrshire sits, or rather sat, on large coal deposits, now mostly worked out or abandoned as 'uneconomical', and at the height of the Industrial Revolution around the mid 1800's, this busy area of over 100 acres was an important producer of coal, ironstone and limestone. Up to eight furnaces blasted away day and night, and 1400 people were employed here.

The open-air industrial museum tells the story of the industries, the workers and their families (it's said that the bar in the Company Store was the longest bar in Ayrshire!), and it's officially the Best Preserved example of a Victorian ironworks in the whole of Europe; indeed, many of its buildings are listed as Ancient Monuments. And it's not as boring as it may sound - much modern technology has been utilised to make the site interesting, exciting and informative for all the family. There's loads to do, and you could spend the whole day here.

In the Visitor Centre is the recreated Victorian Manager's office, where the recreated Victorian Manager will welcome you on video. He will tell you a bit about the ironworks, and invite you to view The Mary Gallagher Experience, a well-produced short film which relates the 19th and early 20th Century story of the works, through the eyes of young Mary, a newly-wed from 1947.

Behind is the Furnace Play Tower for 7-12 year olds, where they can pretend to be a lump of coal or ore or limestone going through the various processes involved in the "furnace". They can choose to be turned into either pig iron or slag, depending on which parts they go through. (Don't know whether it'd turn me on, but kids seem to enjoy that sort of thing. "Today children, we're going to be a lump of slag........" Yeah, sure!)

Recently, Dunaskin has been announced as the new headquarters of the Ayrshire Railway Preservation Group. They plan to have their collection of railway memorabilia and other artefacts on show here. As if that news wasn't good enough, the local Conservation Trust is planning to build a Rally Racing go-cart track here, and has ideas for further developments.

On other parts of the site, there is the Craigton Mine Experience, where original mining tools and machinery are on show; Chapel Row Cottage, a miner's cottage which has been beautifully recreated in 1914 style; workshops with working machinery; and walks through the attractive, wooded Dunaskin Glen, an official S.S.S.I. - Site of Special Scientific Interest. Also in the Visitor Centre you will find the coffee shop, restaurant and gift shop, and information on guided and audio tours.

On Sundays during July and August, some of the steam locomotives are fired up at the nearby Industrial Railway Centre (see next entry.), but check first for details.

Note: since most of the exhibits are in the open, sensible shoes are advised, as there is quite a bit of walking involved. There is disabled access, and guide dogs are allowed. Scottish Tourist Board Commended.

HOW TO GET THERE
The museum is on the A713 Ayr to Dumfries road, about 12 miles (19 km) from Ayr. Nearest railway station is in Ayr. From Burns Statue Square outside the station, there is a #51 bus every 15 mins, or every hour on Sundays.

OPENING TIMES
April-end October, 10-5 daily.
Other months by request.

CHARGES
££, and concessions.

42
Scottish Industrial Railway Centre
Minnivey Colliery, Dalmellington
Tel: Doon Valley Heritage office - 01292 531144 office hours, Secretary 01292 313579 evenings & weekends.

This centre is on the site of the former colliery, very near to the Dunaskin Experience, and is a must for railway anoraks - sorry, buffs - of all ages. If, like me, the very thought of steam engines makes your eyes glaze over, don't let it - it'd be a shame if you didn't visit here, because it's well worth it. The museum is full of railway artefacts, memorabilia and vintage documents, and there is a wide-ranging collection of steam locomotives and rolling stock of many types, some up to eighty years old. My youngest grandson, who's into engines, thinks this place is Heaven.

The BIG attraction of this place though, is the Steam Days, some Sundays in May and June, and each Sunday in July and August, when, subject to availability, you won't fail to be excited and exhilarated by a ride behind a real smelly, smoky, noisy steam engine along the Centre's half-mile track. There are guided tours and explanatory displays, and you can browse in the gift shop or buy refreshments. Disabled access.

HOW TO GET THERE

The Centre is just a short distance past Dunaskin (see previous entry) on the A713, and about 14 miles (22.5 km) from Ayr. Travel arrangements as for Dunaskin.

OPENING TIMES

Static displays every Saturday from early June to late September. Steam Days as detailed above, 11-4.30, but phone first for precise dates.

CHARGES

££, and concessions

Left:
The Scottish Industrial Railway Centre is home to a wide array of steam memorabilia and is located just a short distance from 'The Dunaskin Experience' where this locomotive can be seen.

43
Cathcartston Visitor Centre
Dalmellington
Tel: 01292 550633

At the beginning of the 19th Century, one of Scotland's principal industries was the export of cotton manufactured goods, but the hand weaving industry collapsed because of the shortage of cotton caused by the American Civil War. Hand loom weaving in finer fabrics continued though, and some weavers' cottages are preserved in this centre.

In the recreated kitchen, you will see how a typical weaver and his family lived. The loom is set up in the room, (the loom in the room?) and figures depict the different family members. Actors' voices emanate from each figure to explain their daily lives.

Changing displays reflect the evolution and importance of the coal and iron industries of the area, and the general history of the Doon Valley.

There's even a section on the history of the prize-winning Dalmellington Silver Band, and a collection of many old books, photographs and maps.

There are also microfiche files for research into local family histories.

HOW TO GET THERE

Dalmellington is on the A713, about 14 miles (22.5 km) southeast of Ayr. The Centre is just off the Square in the centre of town.

OPENING TIMES

Mon-Fri, 10-4.30, all year.

CHARGES

Free

44
Loch Doon Castle
Near Dalmellington
Tel: 0131 668 8600 (Historic Scotland)

There are magnificent views surrounding this castle. It is either 13th or 14th Century, depending on who you ask. Whichever it is, not much else is known about it. Originally, it was on a small island in the loch, but when the hydro-electric scheme's reservoir was created in the 1930's, the castle was moved stone by stone to its present site to prevent it being lost to the rising waters. We know that in 1303, Sir Christopher Seton fled here after the defeat of Robert the Bruce in battle at Methven. However, he and the castle were promptly handed over to the English by Gilbert de Carrick, governor of the castle. Sir Christopher, the Bruce's brother-in-law, was hanged as a traitor, but the Bruce appears to have taken no revenge against de Carrick. There were sieges against the castle in the 14th Century and again in the 16th, when finally, it was destroyed by a major fire. The nine feet (3 m) wide portcullis gate was discovered in the loch many years ago, and when it froze over one winter, an attempt was made to recover the gate. However, it proved to be too heavy, the ice broke, and it plunged again to the bottom, where it lies to this day, presumably.

An aerial gunnery school was established here during the First World War. At the north end of the loch opposite the dam, you will see concrete blocks, the foundations of a track which carried the targets at which the trainee gunners fired. There were also plans for barracks, a railway, stables, an airfield, even a 400-seat cinema, but the idea was ill-conceived due to the boggy ground and the often rotten weather. That, and the high costs involved, led to the £3 MILLION project being abandoned.

Another 'brilliant' idea for the area was in 1978, when the nuclear industry applied for permission to dig a big hole in a nearby hill, in order to fill it with the radioactive waste products of most of Europe. Fortunately, the outcry from locals and Conservation bodies was such that permission was not granted, a famous victory of its day. Unfortunately, the nuclear industry is still looking for places to dump its waste in this area, apparently because of the high granite content of the hills, and newspapers sometimes refer to Scotland as the 'Nuclear Dustbin of Europe'. There are also many and repeated complaints of jets disturbing the population and the wildlife, particularly deer herds, as they practise low-flying bombing runs in the hills. (The jets, not the deer, silly!)

Fishing in Loch Doon is, surprisingly, free, and an experienced angler should have little difficulty landing a nice trout. I'm told that there is also a rare fish called the char here, so good luck! Hill walking is very popular in this area, but you should take great care - even in Summer, the weather can turn very bad very rapidly, and you should always have the correct clothing and equipment. Visitor information, toilets and refreshments are available from the kiosk at the dam.

HOW TO GET THERE	**OPENING TIMES**
Follow the signs to Loch Doon from the A713, just south of Dalmellington. The castle is at the southern end of the loch.	Access is at all reasonable times
	CHARGES
	Free

Loch Doon near Dalmellington is a Forestry Commission area with other lochs and reservoirs nearby. It is truly a beautiful place.

The castle was moved stone-by-stone from an island in the middle of the loch in the 1930's when a hydro-electric scheme created the reservoir.

For full details see chapter 44 in this book.

Above:
The Burns House Museum at Mauchline. See chapter 50B for details.

Below:
A panoramic shot over the Clyde Islands with Hunterston Power Station (chapter 14) prominent on the coastline.

45
Sorn Castle
Sorn, by Mauchline
Tel: 01505 612124
Fax: 01505 613304

Sorn Castle stands in a magnificent setting on a cliff above the River Ayr, near the conservation village of Sorn, which is always kept in a tidy and flowery condition.

The original castle keep, named from the Gaelic word 'sron', meaning promontory, dates from the 14th Century. Additions in the same local pink sandstone were made in the 15th, 18th and 19th centuries, so many additions in fact, that the original building has all but disappeared. It has a Royal connection too, King James VI having had a sort of Weekend Bargain Break here in 1598. For all of the 20th Century, the castle has been a family home for the McIntyre family, and contains many fine examples of Scottish art, furniture, china and silverware.

The woods and grounds were laid out partly in the mid-1600's when roads were built and moorland was cultivated, but what we see now was done mainly in the

18th Century, and the extensive grounds boast an impressive collection of trees, rhododendrons and azaleas.

There are attractive riverside walks and all the fresh air you could want.

HOW TO GET THERE

Sorn is on the B743, 4 miles (6.4 km) east of the A76 at Mauchline.

OPENING TIMES

Being a family home, limited.
Mid July to mid August, 2-4, or by appointment.
Grounds open April 1-October 30.

CHARGES

Castle, £££

46
Crossraguel Abbey
Near Maybole
01655 883113

Pronounced "Cross-**ray**-gool", the ruins of the Abbey are under the care of Historic Scotland. It was founded around the middle of the 13th Century by Duncan, Earl of Carrick, being helped along the way over the next few generations with extensions and additions by Robert the Bruce and his descendants, indeed, the Bruce was probably baptised here. Robert III signed the great Crossraguel Charter, giving the Abbot jurisdiction over practically everything and everybody for ever, and the power to act as judge and jury in cases of serious crime.

It is said that if you want to know how your average medieval monastery was laid out, you should look no further than Crossraguel. The Abbey was very large, with buildings spread over a wide area, indeed, it was grand enough to have grain mills, breweries and even its own mint. It seems to have coped with the changes of the Reformation Act of 1560 quite well. This was when the status and power of the Roman Catholic Church was overturned forcefully, abbeys were destroyed, and Presbyterianism was established. Thanks to the protection of the Earl of Cassillis though, Crossraguel was still a working monastery right up until about 1617.

Extensive excavations have been made, and the ruins or foundation walls of many parts of the Abbey are now clearly visible, including the cloisters, chapter house, refectory and domestic buildings and offices.

With explanatory plaques describing the various buildings, it is easy to get a pretty good idea of what daily life at the Abbey must have been like. In the walls of the Abbot's Tower can be seen gun loops, basically holes for guns to be poked through, which tends to suggest that the Abbot had always to expect a bit of trouble from time to time, and that he was prepared to shoot first and ask questions later.

The Abbey's name appears to come from 'Cross of Riaghail', referring to a large standing stone cross, now lost.
There are leaflets, toilets, souvenirs, disabled access and parking, but no refreshments.

Scottish Tourist Board Commended.

HOW TO GET THERE

The Abbey is 2 miles (3 km) south of Maybole on the A77, south of Ayr.

Nearest railway station Maybole. Buses go from Ayr to Girvan via Maybole.

OPENING TIMES
Apr 1-Sept 30,
Mon-Sat 9.30-6.30, Sun 2-6.30.
Closed Thursday pm and Fridays.

CHARGES
££

47
Blairquhan Castle
Straiton, Maybole KA29 7LZ
Tel: 01655 770239 Fax: 01655 770278
Email: enquiries@blairquhan.co.uk
Website : www.blairquhan.co.uk

Pronounced "Blair Kwan", there has been a settlement of sorts on this site since the mid 1300's. The house we see today was built by Sir David Hunter Blair in 1824, in the then highly fashionable and grand Tudor-Gothic style. He acquired the 2000-acre estate at a bit of a knockdown price, as the previous owners had lost most of their wealth in a bank crash.

The large 'castle', a family home, is set on the edge of a natural plateau, and earns its bread and butter by being a venue for conferences, corporate meetings, weddings, even private house parties when you can have the whole place to yourself, but twenty or so of its rooms are viewable by the public for a short season.

Sir David collected many fine examples of the Scottish Colourists school, but I'm afraid I'm too much of a Philistine to appreciate fully what that means. (Images of kilted men Painting By Numbers come to mind, but that can't be right!) I do know, however, that it is a valuable collection, and is well worth seeing. There is also a fine collection of antique furniture and a family museum.

It has spectacular and beautiful grounds, with sheltered, formal, walled gardens with original glasshouses, icehouse, mushroom tunnel, and a fine pinetum, or collection of pine trees, including a Giant Sequoia brought as a seed in about 1860 from North America. In the brief open season, quite a few interesting events take place in the grounds, including archery displays, model aeroplane flying, and sometimes, battle re-enactments. There are guided tours in English and French, and there are explanatory displays, gift shop, and refreshment and picnic areas. Disabled access.

Rooms with four-poster beds are available on a half- or full-board basis at reasonable-for-a-special-occasion prices, and there are seven attractive cottages in the grounds available for holiday rental.

HOW TO GET THERE

Blairquhan is deep in the countryside south of Ayr. From Ayr, take the A713 to Dalmellington. There, turn west onto the B741. Blairquhan is just after the B7045 turnoff on the right.
There are other ways from the A77, but consult a good map!

OPENING TIMES

A very short season, mid July-mid August, 1.30-4.30 daily. Tues-Sun.
Phone to check precise dates.
Gardens open same days.

CHARGES

£££, plus concessions.

48
Bargany Gardens
Girvan, Ayrshire KA26 9QL
Estate office: 01465 871249
Fax: 01465 714191

Bargany House was built in 1681, on land owned by the Kennedys, a powerful and long-established family, but has been much extended over the intervening centuries, including having work done by the famous Adam family of Scottish architects.

The Bargany Kennedys were neighbours of their kinsmen the Kennedys of Cassillis, but these two groups didn't get on well at all, and that's putting it mildly. There had been arguments and feuds between them and other local families for many years. The Earl of Cassillis was the one who tortured the Commendator of nearby Crossraguel Abbey to hand over Abbey lands (see entry 'Dunure' and 'Crossraguel Abbey') in 1570, and in 1601, a Cassillis Kennedy assassinated a Bargany Kennedy in an ambush (sounds like the Mafia!). In the nearby town of Ballantrae stands the Kennedy Aisle, a memorial to the murdered Gilbert Kennedy of Bargany.

The present house though, saved from demolition by a public enquiry in 1980, is most famous for its beautiful gardens and woodlands.
In early Spring, it's worth visiting for its magnificent displays of snowdrops and daffodils, and later for the lily pond and many fine specimens of rhododendrons, azaleas, flowering shrubs and rare trees.

Plants from the estate are for sale in the walled garden.

Disabled access.

HOW TO GET THERE

Bargany is off the B734, 4 miles (6.4 km) east of Girvan from the A77 Ayr to Girvan road.
Follow the minor road to Dailly.

OPENING TIMES
March 1- October 31, seven days, 9-7 or dusk if earlier

CHARGES
Free, but donation appreciated.

72

49

Sawney Bean's Cave & Games Loup
Bennane Head, near Ballantrae
Website: www.sawneybean.co.uk
(Warning: there are some pretty gory pictures on the website, so be careful if the kids are around!)

What do you mean, "Who's Sawney Bean?". You've never heard of Ayrshire's famous cannibal? Well, here's the basic, but grisly story. If you've just finished a full Scottish breakfast, skip this bit until later!

Sawney Bean was born around the mid 1600's, and when a young man, met up with a woman who was just like him - lazy, ignorant and violent! They'd been driven out of every community they'd stayed in, so they 'set up home' in a remote sea cave.

They had no money of course, so they turned to robbing and murdering passing travellers. Limbs were smoked over a fire, and hung up around the walls of the cave for later consumption. Entrails and other juicy bits were pickled for snacks.

They were a devoted couple, and did everything together; they fought, they argued, they tormented each other. In between periods of violence, they had fourteen children, who in turn, had another thirty two children, so they were a close family - in fact, they were all **very closely related**, if you get my drift.

Over the course of the twenty five years or so they were in the cave, they were responsible for the disappearance and deaths of perhaps a thousand men, women, and sad to say, children. Nobody knew they were responsible, of course, and despite the lack of evidence, innocent people were blamed and even executed for the crimes, which naturally, kept on happening.

One sunny day - I think it was a Tuesday - they attacked a husband and wife. They killed the wife, but while they were busy drinking her blood, the husband escaped and raised the alarm. Three days later, he returned with soldiers and a pack of blood-hounds. The cave and its horrific contents were discovered, and the whole family was arrested. They were taken to Edinburgh for immediate execution without trial.

No mercy was shown. The men and boys were dismembered and left to bleed to death, the women and girls were forced to watch, then were burned at the stake. At least, that's the story. There are surprisingly few facts to back it up.

Access is free at all reasonable times, **but you must take care** on the path and on the shore, and you must do it at your own risk.

Nearby, is the oddly-named cliff, Games Loup. Loup is a Scots word meaning leap, and the 'ou' is pronounced like the 'ow' in 'cow'.
Anyway, Sir John Cathcart of Carleton, landowner of the parish, had a particularly nasty habit - when he got fed up with his rich wives, he would lure them to this area

on some pretext, perhaps to show them the nice view, and would calmly push them over the cliff, thereby inheriting their wealth.

He got away with this seven times in total. When he invited May Cullean, his eighth wife, to come and look at the nice view, she was suspicious, having heard the gossip. She waited until Sir John's back was turned, and taking revenge for the previous seven, pushed **him** over the cliff.

HOW TO GET THERE

Sawney Bean's cave is on the shoreline at Bennane Head, just north of Ballantrae on the A77 Girvan to Stranraer road. Park in the car park on the sea side of the road. The path starts at the southern end, next to the metal barrier. Take great care descending to the shore, and remember you have to get back up again.
The cave is half hidden behind a large fallen rock, so don't miss it.
Games Loup is a little further north, at a gate in the fence at the roadside, but remember it's a windy cliff, so I don't recommend standing on the edge.

Above:
A view of Loch Doon, near Dalmellington. See chapter 44.

50
Robert Burns
(See the appendix for Burns websites)

There are many places associated with the life and times of Burns, most of them in the general area of Ayr. Note - there is a small collection of Burns artefacts in Dean Castle in Kilmarnock (See also chapters 24, 24a and 25). I'll detail the main ones on the next few pages, but first, for those of you who know little or nothing about the World's Greatest Poet Ever Bar None And Woe Betide Anyone Who Says Different, think shame of yourself. Here's a very potted history.

Burns was born in Alloway, Ayr on January 25, 1759, one of seven children. His family was poor, due to his father's repeatedly unsuccessful attempts to be a tenant farmer. He was a bright lad though, and despite not attending school very regularly, he did well in mathematics, French, Bible study, music and English literature. Burns started poetic writing at an early age, and wrote his first song lyrics, 'Handsome Nell', about a girlfriend, when he was just 15.

He became a tenant farmer just like his father, but was just as unsuccessful. In 1786, when he was on the point of emigrating to Jamaica in disgust, his first collection of poems, The Kilmarnock Edition, was published to critical acclaim. That, and the minor matter of the birth of his first two children to Jean Armour, persuaded him to stay in Scotland. As well as continuing to write and farm, he took a second job as an Exciseman, or tax collector, an important job in those days, since smuggling was rife.

Burns idolised women, and fertilised many of them too! In total, he fathered fifteen children, six of them out of wedlock. A strange kind of farmer, you might think - one who plants his seed and prays for a crop failure...... This lifestyle led to his 'lusty ploughman poet' reputation, although in reality, he was no more guilty than any other red-blooded young man of his time and class.

Over the next few years, his writing, both in English and in lowland Scots, brought him prominence and a kind of fame, but not much money, so he continued to work for the Excise, as well as still trying to run a farm. By all accounts, he was not a physically strong man, and all these things contributed to his ill health and, eventually, his early death.

In order to try to improve their lot, the family moved to Dumfries in 1791, but bad luck and poverty continued to dog them, and Burns became seriously ill in 1796.

He died on 25th July of that year, from what is now recognised as sub-acute bacterial endocarditis, probably caused by blood poisoning following a dental extraction, and not as some books have it, a heart *attack*, or indeed alcoholism, another myth.

Scots, and others, all over the world celebrate the anniversary of his birth each January with Burns Suppers, where his memory is toasted with recitations, songs, and of course, whisky and haggis.

Burns was a clever song collector, arranger, and writer. He played the fiddle and was very familiar with other popular instruments of the day.

During his lifetime, he wrote some of the greatest poems and songs the world has known, amongst them 'Auld Lang Syne' (not **'Zyne'** please, there's no such word!), 'Tam O'Shanter', 'A Man's A Man For A' That', 'To a Mouse', 'John Anderson, My Jo', and my personal favourite Burns love song, 'Ae Fond Kiss'. I read somewhere that his song, 'Green Grow the Rashes', became so universally popular, the Spanish began referring to white Europeans as *gringos*. Plausible, I suppose. I've also read that the best-known tune to 'Auld Lang Syne' (there are two, and I prefer the other one) might be English in origin, possibly from Northumberland!

There are many, many good biographies on his life and work, all available at any good book shop. Some go into great depth, of course, others less so.

One I like is 'Dirt & Deity', by Ian McIntyre, but also check out 'Robert Burns', by Ian Grimble, one of Scotland's most respected historians. It's easily readable with many interesting illustrations.

Right:

Robert Burns memorials are plentiful in this part of Scotland.

This one can be found on the town moor at Irvine.

50a
The Burns National Heritage Park
Alloway, Ayr KA7 4PQ
Tel. 01292 443700   Fax. 01292 441750
Website: www.robertburns.org/park

The Park was established in 1995, and brings together under one banner several separate Burns locations: **Burns' Cottage and Museum, The Tam O' Shanter Experience, Alloway's Auld Kirk, Brig O' Doon, Burns Monument and Gardens.**

Burns' Cottage is a place of sacred pilgrimage for up to 400,000 visitors a year from all over the world. It is to Scotland what Shakespeare's birthplace is to England. The small thatched cottage (re-thatched in Spring 2002) was built by Burns' father, and is where young Robert lived for the first seven years of his life.

Inside, the four rooms have been restored to their condition at the time of his birth in 1759. In the old byre is a short audio-visual presentation of his life, and from there you move through to the other rooms, ending in the kitchen, with period furnishings and authentic fittings, including the actual bed where the poet was born.

Recorded commentaries are played in each room, and foreign language translations are available. In the grounds is a fascinating museum containing about 300 manuscripts and hundreds of love letters in his own hand, including the originals of 'Auld Lang Syne', and 'Tam O'Shanter', as well as personal items like his pistols, snuff box, and shaving razor. There is a shop, a tearoom, full disabled access, attractive gardens and children's play area.

Nearby is **The Tam O' Shanter Experience,** two modern exhibits combining video, stills, sound and lights. One gives a brief history of Burns, the other an exciting and humorous version of perhaps his most famous poem of the eponymous hero's near-fatal attraction to witches dancing around in scanty underwear, having the Devil of a good time.

Burns wrote the poem as a half-serious warning against over-indulgence in drink, and couldn't have used better locations than the adjacent church ruins of **Kirk Alloway** ("Alloway's auld haunted kirk" of the poem), built around 1516, and the **Brig o' Doon**, a possibly 15th Century stone bridge over the river, and the setting for the literally hair-raising climax to the poem. (Its name is also the inspiration of that awful musical, Brigadoon, but there is no direct connection).

If you don't know the poem, it's worth spending some time with it to fully appreciate its highly descriptive, comical, and very visual qualities. William Burnes, the poet's father (Robert dropped the 'e'), is buried in Kirk Alloway churchyard.

The Experience has a really good restaurant and well-stocked gift shop, and is in the Tourist Board's Highly Commended category. In Summer, there is often children's entertainment, actors dramatising Burns' story, music, and even Burns Suppers, where you can visit Kirk Alloway with a lone piper for an enactment of 'Tam O' Shanter'.

The **Monument**, set in attractive gardens adjacent to the Experience, is a large Grecian-style round tower (why?), from where you get great views of the River Doon and the Brig, or bridge, of the poem.

The statue room contains life-sized comical representations of two of Burns' famous characters, the aforementioned Tam O' Shanter and also Souter Johnnie, Tam's drinking pal in the poem.

The Souter was John Davidson, a good friend of the poet. "Souter" is an old Scots word for cobbler, and his house in nearby Kirkoswald can be visited. (See chapter 50d).

Incidentally, the Inn that was the fictitious setting of Tam's drinking exploits is named after him, and can be visited during normal licensing hours. It's situated in Ayr's High Street, just a short distance from the railway station. There is disabled access to the Cottage, the Experience and the Monument.

Right:
The Burns Monument at Alloway.

HOW TO GET THERE

Ayr is on the A77 Glasgow-Stranraer road. Alloway is 2 miles (3 km) south of Ayr on the B7024.

All attractions are signposted from the A77 and the town centre.

There is ample parking at Burns Cottage and the Tam O' Shanter experience. All attractions are within a short walking distance of each other. Nearest railway station Ayr.

Local buses to Alloway. In Summer, there is an open-top service from Ayr bus station.

OPENING TIMES

Burns' Cottage and Museum:
April-October, 9-6 daily.
Nov-March, 10-4 Mon-Sat. 12-4 Sunday.

Tam O' Shanter Experience:
April-October 9-6 daily.
Nov-March 9-5 daily.

Kirk Alloway, Monument & Gardens, Brig o' Doon:
Free access at all reasonable times.

CHARGES

Burns' Cottage ££.
Family tickets available
Tam O' Shanter Experience ££.
Family tickets available.
Combined tickets available.

This is a multi-subject museum in a restored 18th Century street. There are exhibits of Mauchline "boxware" and the history of Mauchline curling tongs - sorry, curling stones.

If you don't know, curling is a bit like lawn bowls, except that instead of rolling bowls on grass, a large round, pill-shaped granite stone, weighing 42 pounds (20 Kg) is slid along ice towards the target. I've tried both bowling and curling, and believe me, curling is much more difficult, requiring complicated tactics, and a high degree of skill and accuracy.

Beginning some time in the late 15th Century, curling was as popular in Scotland as football is today. Recently, there has been a surge in interest, thanks to the fantastic success of the women's team at the Winter Olympics in Salt Lake City. Some 5.5 million people, equivalent to more than the population of Scotland, stayed up late to watch the team win an Olympic Gold Medal with the last stone of the last end of the last match. There is a local connection here, as two of the team live and work in Ayrshire.

These days, there are around 22,000 players in ice rinks all over the country, but originally, a game would start given the slightest excuse, and it was played on frozen ponds, rivers or even just big frozen puddles. Curling stones and other granite products are still manufactured in the town, but unfortunately, the factory doesn't allow visitors. Some granite is obtained from North Wales, but mostly, it comes from Ailsa Craig, a large volcanic rock in the middle of the Firth of Clyde (see chapter 51). The Kay-Bonspeil factory is the only one in the world licenced to take granite from the island.

Boxware is as the name suggests - small wooden boxes in various shapes and sizes, usually made of plane or sycamore. The boxes were varnished and decorated, and used for snuff, matches, spectacles, money and such like, 100 years ago or so. Nowadays, it is highly collectable, and really good examples can change hands for several hundred pounds.

Also in the museum is the actual room in which Burns and his wife Jean Armour first lived after their marriage in 1788. There are period furnishings, fittings and artefacts. Guided tours are available by appointment, and there are explanatory displays and a gift shop. There is some disabled access.

Across the road is the building which was Nance Tinnock's Tavern. How fortunate Burns was, to have a boozer opposite his house! Inside are explanatory displays, and information about the poet.

Nearby are other Burns-related locations. Mauchline Parish Church is the setting for his poem, "The Holy Fair", and its churchyard is the last resting place of some of his friends. It also has the graves of four of his children who died in infancy. They are clearly marked with plaques. Poosie Nansie's tavern, another of his 'locals', and the setting for "The Jolly Beggars", is opposite the church. Nearby, Mossgiel Farm where he was a tenant farmer for four years, is still a working farm today, but is not open to the public. There is also the fascinating but decidedly odd-looking National Burns Memorial Tower, now a Tourist Information Centre, but which looks as if it's been sliced off the end of a reject Disneyland castle.

HOW TO GET THERE

Mauchline is on the A76 Kilmarnock-Dumfries road, or take the A70 Ayr-Cumnock road, and turn north onto the A76. The Museum is in Castle Street, a narrow cobbled street just off the crossroads at the traffic lights in the centre of town. The Church and Poosie Nansie's are around the corner in Loudoun Street, where there is a good car park. The Memorial Tower is on Kilmarnock Road, at the north end of the town. It's a tall slim red sandstone building standing on its own, and you can't miss it. The nearest railway and bus stations are at Ayr and Kilmarnock.

OPENING TIMES

Museum:
Easter weekend then
May 1-September 30.
Tuesday-Saturday 12-5.
Sunday 2-5.

Closed Mondays.

CHARGES

Museum £

Above:
Poosie Nansie's Tavern in Mauchline, the setting for Burns' "The Jolly Beggars".

50c
Bachelors' Club
Sandgate Street, Tarbolton KA5 5RB
Tel. 01292 541940.

(This has nothing to do with an Irish singing trio, popular in the 60's with hits like *'Marie'*, *'Diane'*, and *'Charmaine'*!)

Life in 18th Century rural Scotland was hard, unless you were a landowner or other member of the gentry. For most ordinary folk, pleasures were simple and few and far between, but nearly every young man with an education would meet with his peers for drinks, storytelling and discussions. Then, as now, these discussions invariably 'sorted' the problems of the world in a single night.

In Burns' case, these witty and stimulating arguments led, in 1780, to the formation of the Bachelors' Club, a literary and debating society which met in this still-thatched house. Burns was its first chairman, and its hand-written Constitution, which without question is written in his style, still survives. Membership was restricted to sixteen, and discussion and discourse was allowed on any subject other than "disputed points of religion".

In keeping with its Gentleman's image, swearing, rough language and indecent talk were prohibited, as was the revelation of any of the club's activities or business to outsiders. The Club provided Burns with his first audience, and taught him the skills of public speaking, skills which he put to good use when he became a regular guest at posh Edinburgh *soirees* in later years.

The room on the upper floor was also used for dancing lessons, a necessary talent, as every young gentleman was expected to be able to dance with the ladies. Conveniently, it was connected to the inn next door by an outside staircase, so the thirst generated by dancing lessons or debate was easily and quickly quenched.

The building is now under the care of the National Trust for Scotland, and contains explanatory displays and period furnishings.

Disabled access is to ground floor only, and toilets are not suitable for wheelchairs.

HOW TO GET THERE

Turn off the A76 south of Kilmarnock onto the A719 and follow the signs, or turn off the A77 north of Ayr onto the A719, and follow the signs. The Club is a white painted building with red shutters and doors in the centre of the village, half hidden round the corner from the chemist's and the Post Office. The nearest railway and bus stations are at Ayr, then it's local buses.

OPENING TIMES

April 1-Sept 30,
1.30-5.30 daily.
Weekends in Oct,
1.30-5.30

CHARGES

££. Concessions.
National Trust members

50d
Souter Johnnie's Cottage
Main Road, Kirkoswald, KA19 8HY
Tel. 01655 760671

'Souter' (sooter) means 'shoemaker' in Scots, and was the nickname given to John Davidson, a good friend and drinking companion of Burns.
He was immortalised in *Tam O' Shanter* thus:

> *".... And at his elbow, Souter Johnnie,*
> *His ancient, trusty, drouthy, crony;*   (thirsty; friend)
> *Tam lo'ed him like a very brither;*   (loved; brother)
> *They had been fu' for weeks thegither...."* (full, drunk; together)

This thatched, stone-floored cottage of 1785 where he lived and worked, has been well preserved and is now under the care of The National Trust for Scotland.

On display are some Davidson family possessions, including box beds, furniture, the family Bible and his tools in his reconstructed workshop, along with other Burns memorabilia and explanatory displays. In the attractive cottage garden is a restored alehouse (an alehouse in the garden?? I want one!), where life-size statues of the Souter, Tam O' Shanter, the innkeeper and Kirkton Jean, the innkeeper's wife, can be seen in poses suggested by the poem.

Tam is wearing the type of wide, flat, round cap that now bears his name. Explanatory leaflets are available in French, Dutch, German and Italian.

Disabled access to ground floor. Scottish Tourist Board commended.

The hero of the poem was also based on a real person, Douglas Graham, tenant of nearby Shanter Farm, and owner of a boat called *Tam O' Shanter,* and you can visit the graves of Graham and Souter Johnnie in the churchyard across the road.

The Tam O' Shanter Inn, the fictitious setting for Tam's drinking spree, is now a restaurant in Ayr's High Street, near the railway station.

HOW TO GET THERE

Kirkoswald is on the A77 Ayr-Stranraer road, 4 miles (6.4 km) south of Maybole. Use the car park at the south end of the village.

The nearest railway station is at Maybole. Buses go from Ayr or Girvan.

OPENING TIMES

April 1- Sept 30,
11.30-5 daily.
Weekends only in October,
11.30-5.

CHARGES

££. Child and family concessions.
Trust members free.

50e
Ellisland Farm
Holywood Road, Auldgirth, Dumfries DG2 0RP
Tel: 01387 740426
Email: friends@ellislandfarm.co.uk
Website: www.ellislandfarm.co.uk

Dumfries is not in Ayrshire, but is easily and quickly reached, and has interesting and important connections with Burns' story that you should visit, so for that reason, I've included three of them in this section.

Burns took over this land in 1788, and had the farmhouse built, eventually. Even in those days, people had trouble with builders! He tried hard to make a good go of it, but the land was poor, and two bad harvests left him practically penniless and ill. Within a few years, he was ready to give up completely.

He wrote to his brother Gilbert that, *"....this farm has undone my enjoyment of myself.....it is a ruinous affair.....let it go to hell!"*. Needing a regular income though, he became an Exciseman, a sort of tax collector, in nearby Dumfries. Conditions were tough, though. He was riding sometimes 200 miles (320 km) a week on Excise duties as well as working on the farm, and he wrote that he was suffering from, *"...an incessant headache, depression of spirits, and all the truly miserable consequences of a deranged nervous system."*. Despite these hard times, Burns wrote over 130 poems and songs at Ellisland, including some of his most famous works - 'Auld Lang Syne' (remember - not **Z**yne!) and 'Tam O' Shanter'.

The farmhouse has been painstakingly restored to its original layout, and is the only one of four farms where he lived that has been preserved for public viewing.

On display are some of his personal possessions - his mirror, his fishing rod, some of his books, original manuscripts, and oddly, a poem scratched on a pane of glass. There are guided tours, and the friendly curator will tell you all you need to know. Also, there are explanatory displays and a riverside walk, where it is said, he composed his famous poem about Tam and his secret observations of the witches' Dirty Dancing.

In the farm's granary are further displays of his possessions, and some of those of Jean, his wife. It also plays a film of the story of Burns' tenancy on a wide-screen TV.

HOW TO GET THERE

The farm is situated on the A76 about 6 miles (9.6 km) north of Dumfries.

The nearest railway station is Dumfries, then a local bus will get you there.

OPENING TIMES

Easter-Sept,
10-1 & 2-5 Mon-Sat.
2-5 Sundays
1st Oct-weekend before Easter,
10-1 & 2-5, Tues-Sat.

CHARGES

Adults £ + concessions.

Burns lived and worked as an Exciseman in Dumfries from the end of 1791 until his death in July 1796.

This award-winning visitor centre, in a beautifully-converted 18th Century watermill, details Burns' connections with the town. On display are original documents and items relating to Burns, and a terrific scale model of the town at the time he lived there. When Burns died in 1796 (see next entry), he was buried in a fairly plain grave, but his remains were moved to the present mausoleum twenty years later.

In the visitor centre is a panel with a fascinating, if slightly ghoulish, account of the reburial, with a plaster cast of his skull.

Also in the building is an impressive film presentation with induction loop for the hard of hearing, a bookshop and gallery.

Explanatory leaflets are available in French, German, Spanish, Italian, Japanese and also Russian, not so unusual when you know that Burns is very big in Russia. (The Moscow Burns Supper is one of the most prestigious in the world, and those on the Burns Supper speaking circuit are highly honoured to get an invitation.) In fact, there are Burns Clubs all over the world, even one in Zambia!

There is also a gift shop, café, and full disabled access. Scottish Tourist Board Commended.

Right: Burns Mausoleum

HOW TO GET THERE

Dumfries is at the end of the A76, about 60 miles (96.5 km) southeast from Ayr. Alternatively, follow the signs to Dumfries from various turnoffs on the M74. Trains run from Glasgow.

The Centre sits on its own on the south bank of the river in the central part of the town.

OPENING TIMES

April-September,
10-8 Mon-Sat. 10-5 Sunday.
October-March,
10-5 Mon-Sat.

CHARGES

Admission free.
Audio-visual theatre £.
Concessions.

50g
Burns House Dumfries
24 Burns Street, Dumfries DG1 2PS
Tel: 01387 255297
Website: www.dumfriesmuseum.demon.co.uk

Burns and his family lived in this simple house for only three years before his death in 1796. It's a major attraction for enthusiasts from all over the world, and has been kept much as it was in his time. It was officially opened on the anniversary of his birth in 1935 by Jean Armour Burns Brown, his great granddaughter. There are many Burns relics and possessions:- the very chair in which he sat writing poems and songs, items of equipment he used in his Excise duties, his gun, whisky glass, lots of original letters and manuscripts, and a famous and priceless Kilmarnock First Edition of his collected works.

The museum is undoubtedly fascinating, but there is an air of sadness about it, as it was in this house that, dying from bacterial endocarditis (inflammation of the heart), and with his wife Jean Armour on the verge of childbirth, he wrote to his father-in-law:

"Do, for Heaven's sake, send Mrs Armour here immediately. My wife is hourly expecting to be put to bed. Good God! What a situation for her to be in, poor girl, without a friend! My medical friends would almost persuade me that I am better, but I think and feel that my strength is so far gone that the disorder will prove fatal to me."

These were the last words Burns wrote. Soon after, he slipped into a coma, and three days later, he died. He was 37. As his burial service was taking place, Jean was giving birth to their ninth child, a son. How sad. You should hope to visit when it's quiet, and there are no noisy children there.

There are explanatory displays, leaflets in French, German, Spanish, Italian, Japanese and Russian, and a gift shop. No wheelchair access. Scottish Tourist Board Commended.

If you wish to pay your respects, visit his mausoleum in nearby St Michael's churchyard, and marvel at the representation of 'The Ploughman Poet'. Also interred here are Jean and five other members of their family.

HOW TO GET THERE

The house is on the north side of the river, at the southern end of the High Street.
Your best landmark is the suspension bridge. It's not terribly well signposted, so you may need to ask directions. Even with the map in the Dumfries Burns Trail leaflet, I got lost!

OPENING TIMES

April-Sept,
10-5, Mon-Sat.
2-5 Sunday.
Oct-March,
10-1, 2-5, Mon-Sat.

CHARGES

Free

Ailsa Craig, from the Gaelic *ailsse creag*, meaning 'fairy rock', can be seen from all parts of the Ayrshire coast, not surprising, considering it's 1110 feet high (338 m).

Looking like a giant crusty bread roll, it's technically a granite volcanic plug about 1300 yards long (1100 m) and about 900 yards (820 m) across. It's about 10 miles (16 km) off the coast, roughly halfway between the mainland and Ireland, hence its moniker, "Paddy's Milestone".

What even some locals probably don't know is that it's the home of the third largest gannet colony in the world, with about 70,000 birds on average. For that reason, it is a registered Site of Special Scientific Interest, maybe even a European Special Protection Area.

Granite was mined from Ailsa Craig from the early 1800's to about 1971 for making kerb stones and curling stones, though recently, there has been a bit of a revival of quarrying, with one factory being licenced to take the granite. The items are made in Mauchline (see entry, "Burns House Museum"), and exported all over the world.

From the harbour at Girvan, cruises to the island can be made aboard the *MFV Glorious* (phone 01465 713219 for details), or the *Rachael Clare*, (phone 01294 833724), weather permitting. A four-hour trip costs about £9 per adult, but note that the boats are only about 30 ft long (10 m), and not entirely covered, so whatever the weather, you will need protection.

The Clyde can be pretty lumpy, so bear that in mind, too. If the sea is calm, you can land and spend some time on it, enough to have a look at the ruined miners' cottages - no, that should read the miners' ruined cottages - the old narrow-gauge railway running from the quarry, the lighthouse dating from 1886, and the old foghorn. (There's a mother-in-law joke in there, but I daren't make it!)

In its heyday, the island's population was 29, made up of miners, their families, and lighthouse keepers. Their cottages were sold in 1999, complete with their own helicopter pad. At the time of writing, there are plans to open the cottages as luxury holiday homes for rent, but some conservation groups are opposed to the idea.

It is known that Ailsa Craig was owned by the Abbey at Crossraguel in the early 1400's, when apparently, ambitious, and therefore recalcitrant abbots were sent here to cool off a bit. In those days, abbots weren't necessarily men of holy orders, so it must have been a busy place.

Nowadays, the really energetic visitor may have a chance to climb to the top, via the path that passes a ruined castle.
The castle had three storeys and was built by the powerful Hamilton family in the late

1500's, after Philip of Spain tried to capture the island for himself.

Why on earth a Spanish king wanted a big rock in the middle of the Firth of Clyde, I can't imagine. It's nice in its own way, but it's hardly Gibraltar. Control over shipping in the Clyde? Ah yes, that's it.

The exporting of birds' feathers was an important industry in days gone by, and it is said that Robert Burns ordered a quantity for a new bed when he married Jean Armour.

Other writers have been influenced by Ailsa Craig as well, and both Keats and Wordsworth have mentioned it in their work. Oddly, Burns makes only fleeting mention of it.

David Craig, a native of south Ayrshire, was one of the first settlers in a remote part of Ontario, Canada, in the mid 1800's, and he named a town after his favourite island.

More information on Ailsa Craig can be found at the McKechnie Institute in Dalrymple Street in Girvan.

Above:
Ailsa Craig is clearly seen in the sea south of Holy Isle, approximately 10 miles off the Ayrshire coast.

52
The Isle of Arran
Websites: *www.arran.net*
www.arransites.co.uk

(Before we go any further, this Arran is spelt with two r's and has nothing to do with woolly jumpers lately beloved of finger-in-the-ear folk singers. These garments come from the Aran Isles off the west coast of Ireland. However, you can buy Aran jumpers on Arran. Clear?)

Arran (from the Gaelic for 'peaked island') is often described as Scotland in Miniature, because it contains all the geographical features found elsewhere in Scotland - craggy mountains, heather-covered hills and moors, fertile lowland plains and sandy beaches, not to mention stunning views, sheep, whisky, real beer, narrow roads and midgies! It is also said that you can get all four seasons in one day here.

This is probably true - the weather can be different from one end to the other, or from one side to the other - but it is also true that Arran's weather can be much better than on the mainland, particularly on the sheltered, albeit wetter, eastern side. On days of warm sunshine, and there are many, it can be like a Mediterranean island.

Up to 300,000 visitors return to Arran again and again for its wild, empty hills, attractive villages of whitewashed cottages, fresh air, and slow pace of life. There is no rush hour here, no traffic jams, no polluted air, no hassle, but loads of easily-obtainable peace and quiet. I've been visiting Arran regularly for a number of years now, and I'm always captivated by the island's beauty and relaxing air. You will be too.

The island lies about 12 miles (19 km) off the Ayrshire coast, is about 26 miles long by 12 miles across (42 km by 19 km), and its permanent population is around 4600.

It can be reached by a large car ferry from Ardrossan in 55 minutes, or by smaller ferry in Summer from Claonaig on the Mull of Kintyre. Although quite expensive, it's worth taking the car to be able to sample all the island's attractions and explore all its fascinating little corners. The main ferry runs all year, and it's best to book ahead, particularly at weekends and peak holiday times. (See appendix.)

The ferry from Ardrossan is the modern *Caledonian Isles.* This ship was built specially for this run, and sails several times daily, more often in summer of course. It's a comfortable ship, and its stabilisers nearly always make for a smooth crossing. As I said, it's expensive - an average car with two adults and two kids will cost between £60 and £70 return at 2002 prices (under 5's are free), but your tickets are valid for five days. Lots of people bring sandwiches and eat them on deck, or more interestingly, in the ship's cafeteria, which I think says something.... Prices at the licenced bar, though, are sensible. If you're relying on public transport, trains run from Glasgow, Largs or Ayr, and go right to the ferry terminal. Buses meet all ferries and go all over the island.

Arran's been occupied for around 9,000 years, and in 1999, the site of a small settlement was discovered near Lamlash when new water pipes were being laid. Archeologists have dated the site to around 5000 years old, making it probably the oldest 'house' in the UK. Like many parts of Highland and Island Scotland, Arran was affected by the Clearances of the 18th and early 19th centuries. It was a kind of Ethnic

Cleansing, and is a shameful part of Scotland's history. These were the times when the rich landlords who owned vast areas of hills and moor realised that, since sheep were far more profitable than people, and a lot less bother, the land should be cleared of houses, even whole communities, and if necessary, forcibly by troops. Being deprived of their ability to earn a living, emigration was the only answer for most people.

In Lamlash, there is a memorial to some of those 300 or so who left the island, erected by their descendants. A plaque tells how the families left in 1829 aboard the brig *Caledonia* for Megantic County, Quebec. Their minister had preached to them for the last time from the small, natural mound opposite the memorial, but thereby hangs another tale. A few years ago, the local Council was renovating and tidying the area, work which involved levelling and grassing over the rather uneven and stony ground. Imagine their chagrin when it was pointed out by concerned locals that they'd flattened the very mound mentioned in the soon-to-be-unveiled plaque. A squad of grinning workmen with big shovels was quickly despatched, and hey presto, the mound (or something akin to it) was recreated, as-near-as-makes-no-real-difference in its original location - or so the locals tell me!

As you approach the main terminal at Brodick (from the Norse *breidr vik* or broad bay), the soaring peak of Goat Fell (from the Norse *geit fiall*, or goat mountain, at 2867 ft or 874 m), the sharp mountain ridges, green fields and white painted cottages beyond the bay will become clearer, and you'll begin to appreciate the island's allure.
Unfortunately, the first close-up view you get is of the Municipal rubbish tip, and a collection of unattractive if not dilapidated industrial buildings and sheds, but look the other way towards the mountains and Brodick Castle.

Brodick itself is nothing to write home about. Its buildings are a haphazard collection of many periods and styles, some very ugly, but its location is spectacular, if not unique. On the hillsides, you'll also see some areas where tree felling has begun in recent years. This is both bad news and good news: it's bad because it doesn't look very nice and will cause some erosion. But it's good news, mainly for jobs, and also because Forest Enterprise, a Government quango, has realised the error of its ways. Instead of its past practice of planting thousands of horrible acres of foreign Christmas trees, smothering or driving out the indigenous plants and wildlife, they will, in future, replant with mixed native trees, thereby recreating a more natural environment for both flora and fauna. Time will tell, of course, but in theory, it works. (Digressing for a moment, this is one reason why films like Braveheart and Rob Roy weren't actually filmed entirely in Scotland - mountain and hill locations were all wrong because Scotland is covered in millions of acres of Sitka spruce, a modern Scandinavian import!)

Perhaps your first stop on the island should be at the Tourist Information Centre at the pier, to arrange accommodation or to get details of what's on, as there are many festivals, galas, and special events throughout the year.

There's a great Folk Festival in June (go to www.arranfolkfestival.org.uk for details), amateur plays running throughout the Summer, and the Highland Games in August are always worth a visit. You'll get full details at the TIC.

If you're staying self-catering, try to buy your provisions from the smaller shops, as many are feeling the pinch since the big Co-op supermarket opened.

52a
Auchrannie Spa Resort
Brodick, Isle of Arran KA27 8BZ
Tel. 01770 302234   Fax. 01770 303300
Email: info@auchrannie.co.uk
Website: www.auchrannie.co.uk

I've included the Auchrannie because its Spa Resort swimming pool is open to non-residents and its other leisure facilities are the best on the island.

The original red sandstone house was the home of the Dowager Duchess of Hamilton, widow of the 12th Duke of Hamilton and Earl of Arran, but it became a Country House Hotel in 1991, and has a Scottish Tourist Board Four Star award.
It's a tastefully decorated and extended period mansion, the luxury rooms having all the trappings you would expect with its status, and has restaurants and bars. Its pool is exclusively for residents. In the grounds of the hotel are eight lodges, ostensibly for timeshare use, but available for short or long breaks. They are luxuriously appointed two or three-bedroom detached lodges with all mod cons included, and with a four star rating. If you're interested, phone for details.

The good news for day visitors, though, is that in 2001, the hotel opened the modern Spa Resort nearby, with a good 20 metre indoor pool, shallow pool for kids, and juice bar open to non-residents, and a huge games hall big enough for two tennis or 4 badminton courts.
You can also relax of course, and enjoy the benefits of the solarium, steam room or aromatherapy massage. Note - the pool will be busy if the weather's bad. The Spa building reminds me of something you might see on holiday in some Mediterranean resort, an image complemented by the palm trees growing outside.

Food is available at Café Cruize, and of course, Bar Cruize is open throughout the day.

HOW TO GET THERE

Going north through Brodick, the road turns sharp right at the golf course clubhouse opposite the sports field, and goes over the river. To get to the Country House Hotel, turn left immediately after the bridge, and follow the narrow road.

To get to the Spa Resort, continue on a few hundred yard/metres, and turn left into Glencloy Road at Jimmi the Barber's wooden shop. Buses will stop at the road end.
If it's a nice day, you can walk from the town.

OPENING TIMES
Pool:
9 to 9.30, Mon-Sat.
9-8.30 Sun.
Adults only Mon & Wed 7.30-9.30.
Games Hall:
9-9, Mon-Sat,
9-8.30 Sun.
Last admission a half hour before closing

CHARGES
Variable, depending on facility.
e.g. Swim, adults ££,
juniors & OAP's £.

52b
Arran Heritage Museum
Rosaburn, Brodick, Isle of Arran KA27 8DP
Tel 01770 302636
Email: tom.macleod@arranmuseum.co.uk
Website: www.arranmuseum.co.uk

This collection of attractive whitewashed cottages and outbuildings was a newly-built farm two hundred years ago, but now, it houses loads of interesting stuff on the social history, archaeology, and geology of the island.

The museum strives to be as authentic as possible, so on the site there's a farmhouse, a smiddy, stables and harness room,   as well as a cottage furnished and equipped as it would have been at the turn of the century. There's a collection of photographs and artefacts from Arran's rural and seafaring past, such as a replica of a Viking ship of seven hundred years ago, and a Bronze Age grave over three thousand years old, complete with pottery grave goods. Stone tools and hunting implements belonging to hunters of the Mesolithic period are on display, too.

The smiddy, which only closed in the 60's, still has all the original forges, bellows and tools in full working order, and you can have a go at pumping the bellows yourself. Horseshoeing demonstrations are given regularly in the summer, as well as occasional displays of spinning and weaving - no, not in the smiddy, silly!

The 2002 season saw the opening of the stable block extension. As well as the museum's computerised archive and database, there is computer access to help visitors in tracing their family's history, or you can ask the museum staff to do this for you, for an extra charge of course!

For details of this service, e-mail: gracesmall@jings.com

There is a splendid tearoom, the Rosaburn Café, riverside picnic area, shop and disabled access.

HOW TO GET THERE

Going north leaving Brodick, the road passes the primary school. The Heritage Museum is soon on the right. Buses stop at the door.

OPENING TIMES
Easter - October, 10.30-4.30 daily.
Winter months, Wednesday only.

CHARGES
Adults £, plus concessions.
Family tickets available.

Arran Aromatics Visitor Centre
The Home Farm, Brodick, Isle of Arran KA27 8BZ
Tel. 01770 302595
Website: www.arran-aromatics.co.uk

This is a busy complex of small shops in what was the large home farm of Brodick Castle.

Arran Aromatics makes environmentally-friendly soaps and bodycare products of many different exotic ingredients and fragrances from all over the world. There's a viewing platform where you can look into the small factory and watch the various cakes, bars, lotions and candles being made, or there's a machine for you to make your own soap. All the finished articles are, of course, for sale, and they make excellent souvenirs or presents.

They're also a great idea for Christmas presents. If you're not in the market for buying, you can happily spend an innocent few minutes sniffing the products, and nobody will look twice at you. In the same building are the Duchess Court shops, where you can buy a wide range of craft items, books and gifts for everyone. There is also a small café that does great coffee and sinful cream cakes.

At one end of the car park is the Island Cheese factory and shop, where you should definitely try their crowdie with garlic and hand-rolled cream cheeses. There is disabled access to the factory viewing areas and all shops.

HOW TO GET THERE

It's on the right hand side of the road, about half way between Brodick and the Castle gates.

OPENING TIMES

Mon-Sat, 9.00-5.30. Sunday 10-5.
Winter hours may vary.

CHARGES

Free

Right:
Arran Heritage Museum. See chapter 52b for full details.

There are many frequent visitors to the Isle of Arran including the Paddle Steamer "Waverley" - pictured above - which includes the island in its varied itinerary. Seals are often seen around the island, particularly in the Blackwaterfoot area (see chapter 52H for details).

Above: A fishing boat heads for Girvan Harbour with the volcanic cap of Ailsa Craig (see chapter 51) on the horizon.
Below: A dramatic view of Holy Isle from Arran.

Above:
The lighthouse at the south end of Holy Isle see chapter 52L) is used as a place of retreat by Buddhist monks from the Samye Ling Monastery in Dumfriesshire.
Below:
Balmichael Visitor Centre (see chapter 52J) is one of Arran's biggest attractions, with leisure activities, crafts and quad bikes.

Left:
Lochranza Castle (see chapter 52G) was probably used as a base for hunting trips by various Scottish kings. Robert The Bruce is said to have been here in the 14th Century.

Below:
The only residents to be found at Lochranza Castle in the 21st Century are sheep and pigeons.

Above:
There are many deer on Arran. This friendly young stag, known to the locals as Angus, is shown near Arran Distillery.

Below:
The picturesque village of Corrie on the east coast of Arran is a haven, both for boats and photographers.

Left:
"The Wedge" at Millport on Cumbrae which at just 47 inches wide is listed as the narrowest house in the UK in the Guinness Book of Records.
See chapter 54.

Below:
Due to their distinctive outline these mountains in the north of Arran are known as "The Sleeping Warrior".

Mount Stuart House (see chapter 53F) on the Isle of Bute was rebuilt with no expense spared after a fire destroyed the original building in the late 19th Century.

52d
Isle of Arran Brewery
Cladach, Brodick, Isle of Arran, KA27 8DE
Tel. 01770 302353   Fax. 01770 302653
Email: info@arranbrewery.co.uk
Website: www.arranbrewery.co.uk

This high-tech microbrewery sits well in its surroundings at Cladach, a small complex of refurbished old buildings north of Brodick, and the site of the original Brodick village. Using cool Arran water and natural ingredients, it produces ales free of artificial preservatives or additives, so it's good stuff.

At present, they have three beers - Dark, a traditional-type Scottish ale; Blonde, a clear, continental type (lager to you and me); and Light, described as a "refreshing session bitter", whatever that means, and very tasty they are, too.

They are on sale at the brewery, or in many outlets throughout the island, so just ask for suppliers. Watch out for the Blonde, though - at 5%, it's pretty strong, as I can testify! In 2000, the brewery's first year of operation, the Blonde won the 'Champion Wheat Beer of Britain' award.

The visitor centre has observation windows, allowing you to see (and smell!) the brewing process at close quarters. Of course, no brewery or distillery visit would be complete without tasting a sample of the products, so there is an opportunity to indulge.

Naturally, there is a shop where you can purchase the beers, the T-shirt, the baseball cap, the bottle opener, etc, etc.

As well as the brewery at Cladach, there is a leatherworker's shop, an outdoor clothing shop, and the Wineport Restaurant and bistro bar.

HOW TO GET THERE

Cladach is north of Brodick, just before the entrance to the Castle. Buses will stop at the road end.

OPENING TIMES

9.30-3.30, Mon, Wed, Thurs, Frid.
9.30-5 Sat.
Closed Tues & Sun.

CHARGES

££, includes a taste of
all three beers.
Children free (they get juice!)

52e
Brodick Castle, Garden & Country Park
Brodick, Isle of Arran KA27 8HY
Tel: 01770 302202   Fax: 01770 302312
Ranger Centre tel: 01770 302462
Website: www.nts.org.uk

The whole lot, including the mountain of Goatfell of 2866 ft (873 m), belongs to the National Trust for Scotland, being gifted to them in 1958 by Lady Jean Fforde (yes, that's two 'f 's), daughter of the 6th Duchess of Montrose.

Somebody, probably Vikings, built a wooden fortress first on this site, but the original stone tower dates from the 13th Century. In the centuries that followed, there were several instances of destruction by invading forces, and rebuilding by new owners, most notably in the late 1600's by Oliver Cromwell, who was a mean hand at the bricklaying, but whose specialities usually lay in the opposite direction (See 'Rothesay Castle').

Even more building took place about 150 years ago, but it all fits together in a pleasing fashion. Its hillside setting is magnificent, with the curve of the bay in front, and the forests and mountain behind, and the late afternoon sun really brings the rosy sandstone to life.

The contents of the house include 16th Century furniture, a jaw-dropping silver collection, and paintings and porcelain collected by the still-influential Hamilton family over many generations. (Sir James Douglas Hamilton of that ilk is an MSP in the Scottish Parliament.)

The large woodland garden is a great place to go on a good day, of which there are many, of course. Laid out in the 1920's, it has a magnificent and internationally-famous rhododendron collection, including species which are well-nigh impossible to grow anywhere else in the UK. They are a sight not to be missed in April, May and early June, when the colours are dazzling and the perfumes will knock you out.

The grounds are undergoing a rolling programme of clearing and replanting in an attempt to eradicate the common purple rhododendron, which has now become a weed, and new paths and areas of interest are always being opened up.

The walled garden of 1710 has been restored to its peak Victorian condition, and is well worth visiting for the roses and borders.

In Summer, there are weekly guided walks of the grounds, which are really worth taking, and evening shore walks are worthwhile too, but DON'T forget your bug spray!

There is a well-stocked shop, where you can also join the National Trust for Scotland, and get free unlimited entry to this and dozens of other properties (See entry, 'Culzean Castle and Country Park').

There is also a licenced restaurant where you can sit outside and hand-feed the chaffinches, an adventure playground, and Ranger service. Information sheets in French, German, Italian, Spanish, Swedish, Norwegian, Japanese and Braille are available. Disabled access is extensive, from the gardens to the Castle's upper floors.

Wheelchairs are available for hire too. When on the island, you must go here.

Tourist Board Commended.

HOW TO GET THERE

Once off the ferry, turn right and head round the bay, then follow the signs, or take the bus at the ferry terminal.

During the summer, a horse and cart or perhaps a vintage bus will do the run right to the door.

OPENING TIMES

Castle:
Apr 1-Jun 30 & Sept 1-Oct 31, 11.30-4.30 daily.
July 1- Aug 31, 11-5
Reception Centre and shop: same dates, 10-5, daily.

Also weekends in Nov & Dec, 11-3.
Garden & Country Park: all year, 9.30-sunset, daily.
Ranger Centre: 9-5 daily.

CHARGES

Castle and Gardens: Adults £££, concessions £££.
Family discounts available.
Gardens only: Adults ££, concessions £.
Family discounts available.

National Trust members free.

52f
Isle of Arran Distillery & Visitor Centre
Lochranza, Isle of Arran KA27 8HJ
Tel. 01770 830264   Fax: 01770 830364
Website: www.arranwhisky.com

This is Scotland's newest Single Malt distillery, and the first on the island for 150 years. (Well, the first legal one, anyway, but don't ask too many questions!) The Queen eventually opened the visitor centre in 1997. I say "eventually", as construction was delayed for a while by nearby nesting Golden Eagles!

Friendly tour guides explain the whole whisky-making process, and there are interactive displays. "Interactive?", you ask, suddenly interested. Yes, you get to taste the finished product, and beautiful it is too. It goes straight to your legs, and causes the interesting phenomenon of getting drunk from the feet up. You're allowed a little water with it, but don't embarrass yourself by asking for it with lemonade, or worse, Coke and a slice of lemon! Amongst affishinon....afichshio....arfeshon...... fans, it is highly respected, and has been compared favourably to the finest of Islay malts.

Arran malt is very pale in colour, slightly sweet on my palate, but it goes down like a torchlight procession! Lovely.

The audio-visual display has been given an unusual twist in that it's fitted out to resemble an 18th Century crofter's cottage, but fortunately, he's always out. There's an induction loop system for the hard of hearing, and foreign language explanations are available in French, Spanish, German, Swedish, Japanese, Italian, etc.

The Distillery Restaurant is an attractive place to have dinner, but I'd recommend booking, especially at weekends. It is recommended by the AA and Taste of Scotland.

There is, of course, a gift shop for well-priced whisky products, gifts and books, and a picnic area. Disabled access.

HOW TO GET THERE

Lochranza is 14 bumpy, twisty, miles (22.5 bumpy, twisty, kilometres) from Brodick at the north end of the island, but after the whisky tasting, the return journey will seem like no distance at all, and the singing and giggling will make time fly by!
Your driver, of course, must be stone cold sober, though. The local police are just as happy to lock up visitors, as locals.
The Distillery is on the left as you enter the village. Buses go from Brodick pier.

OPENING TIMES

All year, tours 10-5, shop 10-6 daily. Restaurant 10-9 daily. Closed Mon eves.

CHARGES

Tours, adults £££, children/concessions ££ Shop access free.

52g
Lochranza Castle
Lochranza, Isle of Arran

Not a great deal is known about this ruined castle, but it was probably built as what was known as a 'hall house' by the McSween family around 1260, and was probably used as a base for hunting trips by various kings of various times. (Is that vague enough for you?) Around the middle of the 15th Century, it was the main Arran residence of the Montgomerie family from Ayrshire (see entry, 'Eglinton Country Park'), who rebuilt it to more or less the present shape. King Robert the Bruce is supposed to have been here, before beginning the campaign which led to the Declaration of Arbroath in 1320 and an independent Scotland. Part of this document, also called the Declaration of Independence states,

"For so long as a hundred of us remain alive, we will yield in no least way to English dominion. For we fight, not for glory, nor riches, nor honour, but only for freedom, which no good man surrenders but with his life".

Little did The Bruce know that, around 678 years later, an American/Australian actor with a strangely modern Glasgow accent would rewrite the speech, thus avoiding copyright problems, paint his face blue, and make a hit movie out of it. Perhaps Bruce was even staying at Lochranza when he allegedly had the famous encounter with a spider when out for a walk one day (See entry, "King's Cave"), but he didn't sign the visitor's book, so we don't know for sure. A violent storm demolished a large part of the building in 1897, making many pigeons and sheep homeless. Yes folks, times were baa-aad! (Sorry!)

It is not unknown for one part of the castle or another to be covered in scaffolding. It gets in the way if you want good photographs, but it does mean that the fabric of the building's being kept in good nick.

The castle features in Sir Walter Scott's novel, 'Lord of the Isles'. I read somewhere that the castle is also said to have been the model for cartoon hero Tintin's adventures in the story, *The Black Island,* although I can't imagine why, as it looks nothing like it.

Seals can always be seen at low tide on the other side of the bay.

HOW TO GET THERE

Once in Lochranza, you can't miss it. It's the big grey square stone thing built on a spit of gravel sticking out into the bay.
Watch out for the sheep guano.
Buses go from Brodick.

OPENING TIMES

Access at all reasonable times. Well, it's normally locked, but a notice at the entrance explains that the custodian and key can be contacted at the village Post Office.

CHARGES

Free

52h
Kinloch Hotel and Blackwaterfoot
Blackwaterfoot, Arran KA27 8ET
Tel. 01770 860444 Fax 01770 860447
Website: www.kinloch-arran.com

The Kinloch started life as a large boarding house in the 50's, and through many changes, including a recently-new top storey, it is now the largest family-run hotel on the island. Apart from its uses as an hotel, it has a decent-sized swimming pool, a family attraction in all weathers. There is also a solarium, sauna, squash court, snooker room and fitness suite.
The rocky shore in front of the hotel is a good place to see seals at low tide.

Nearby is Shiskine Golf and Tennis Club, with tennis courts unsurprisingly, a putting green and all-weather bowling green. The 12-hole golf course has been named by the prestigious Golf World magazine as one of the Best 100 in Britain, and is a favourite of ex-radio DJ and media personality, Chris Evans.

The beach at Blackwaterfoot is probably the best on the island, with safe, shallow bathing and clean sands.
Be aware though that, despite the Gulf Stream, the water can be very cold, even at the height of what is laughingly called Summer.

On the other hand, the beach faces west, so you'll get full advantage of the sun setting over Mulligan's Tyre, the subject of that well-known but infuriating song by Paul McCartney.

Don't forget the picnic!

HOW TO GET THERE
Blackwaterfoot is halfway up (or down) the west coast.
The quickest way is via the String road from Brodick, a road that goes across the island over the hills.
Buses go from Brodick pier.

OPENING TIMES
Hotel pool open all year, 10-5 daily.

CHARGES
Swimming, sauna, solarium and squash ££.
Golf - Adults £££££, junior/child concessions.
More at weekends. Round tickets (play any time) and other rates available.

It's not a 'visitor attraction' in the common sense of the word, but it's worth visiting, if only for the exercise in getting there, and the views you'll get on the way.

Popular tradition states that the cave is the one in which Robert the Bruce watched a spider try, try, and try again to complete a web, giving him the inspiration to continue fighting for Scotland's freedom.

BOOOOM!

What was that? Well, dear reader, that's the sound of another myth exploding. It seems that the spider incident did take place, not in a cave though, but in a forest. And it wasn't The Bruce who witnessed it, but a character called Black Douglas, a Scottish lord, and a fearless guerilla fighter. Being a close friend of The Bruce, he told him the story to inspire him, but when Scottish novelist Sir Walter Scott heard the same story some hundreds of years later, he romanticised it into the nonsense that everyone believes today.

Well, he was a writer after all, but unfortunately, that's not the only piece of Scottish "history" he's responsible for creating. However, what IS true is that King Robert spent some time on Arran forming his campaign, and sulking when it didn't go to plan, so maybe he came here for a walk one day when he couldn't find a cat to kick, and observed the vague Pictish or early Christian carvings in the cave.

There are two ways of reaching it, both by walking. I've done both, so if I can do it, anyone can! One is easy and fairly flat, the other not so flat and maybe a bit longer, or rather, it'll feel like it. The easiest way is to park at the beach in Blackwaterfoot, take the path along the shore, ducking the golf balls, and follow the signs for about a mile and a half. There are a couple of narrower bits over and   between rocks where a little care is needed. On the way, you will pass Drumadoon, a flat-topped hill whose cliffs look like something out of *Close Encounters of the Third Kind*. We know there's an Iron Age fort on top, but it's never been excavated properly, so its exact age can't be determined. In summer, you will see butterflies and dragonflies along the way. This is an easy route, and I've seen people of all ages and physical conditions doing it.

The other way requires slightly more energy. Go north through Blackwaterfoot, and park in the signposted Forest Enterprise car park about a mile outside the town limits. It's then an undulating walk of perhaps an hour or so along the top of heather-covered cliffs, and the views over to the Mull of Kintyre and beyond are magnificent.

At the end, you scramble down a narrow and maybe slippy gully, and turn left along the pebbly shore. Wear good shoes for this route (and I don't mean your best shoes!), and be aware that both paths will be a bit boggy in places, unless the weather's been really good for a while.

When you get there, the iron gates across the entrance will probably be locked, but you can still see inside. There's a flat grassy area in front, a good place to have a picnic or a snooze, and it can be a busy place on sunny days.

Note: there are no toilets here, so make your own arrangements!

52j
Balmichael Visitor Centre
Shiskine, Isle of Arran KA27 8DT
Tel/Fax: 01770 860430
Website: www.thebalmichaelcentre.co.uk

This is one of the island's biggest attractions, built in and around converted farm buildings, and is a combination of leisure activities and craft sales outlets for marquetry, wood carving, jewellery, and pottery. Adults will enjoy browsing in the various shops, and there are even antiques for sale in the converted stables. For youngsters there's an adventure playground, and toddlers' indoor playbarn.

Perhaps its most popular attraction though, is the Quad Bikes, where you can zoom around the twisting dirt course, skidding around the corners and flying over the bumps. For younger kids, there's a shorter, flatter course with smaller, slower bikes. All bikes are carefully adjusted, so you can't go dangerously fast. Crash helmets are supplied on both courses.

It's most fun if you go mob handed and when the weather's been dry. The bikes kick up a fair amount of dust, so you finish your ride an interesting shade of beige. To take the dust out of your mouth, retire to the excellent coffee shop for snacks, drinks, or ice cream. If the weather's warm, try to get a table outside, as the courtyard is quite a suntrap. There's full disabled access, except on the quads of course.

Balmichael is also home to the Arran Quad Centre. Each 2-hour guided session will take you on a thrilling quad bike trek in the surrounding hills and woodlands. The minimum age is 16, and all protective clothing is provided - helmets, gloves, jackets, even the boots. Treks take place Apr-Nov 9-6 daily, and Nov-Apr, 9-3 Wed-Sun. Phone for details or email arranquadcentre@yahoo.com

On the way to the Centre from Brodick, stop at the top of the hill and look back. On a good day, you should get a magnificent panorama of the Clyde and the Ayrshire coast. The view of the mountains of north Arran is good too.

Tourist Board Commended.

HOW TO GET THERE

Take the Blackwaterfoot road (String Road) from Brodick for about 7 miles (11 km).
The Centre is on the right at the bottom of the valley.

OPENING TIMES

All year,
Mon-Sat, 10-5 Sunday 12-5

CHARGES

Free. Quad bikes and adventure playground extra.

52k
South Bank Farm Park
Near Kildonan, Isle of Arran KA27 8SH
Tel. 01770 820206

You'll spend an interesting couple of hours here. This is a working 60 acre farm, and there are exotic ducks, geese, rare sheep, goats, poultry, pot-bellied pigs, ponies and pets such as rabbits and guinea pigs. You can feed all the animals except the pigs.

There's a hill trail, with either a short or a long version, where you pass pens with the various animals in them, and terrific views looking south. Don't be surprised if the ducks follow you in a pack - they're after the food which they expect you to have, but they don't understand the word, "SHOO!", and just won't take a telling, so they may try to come home with you.

The sheep are fun to feed too. In the Spring, there'll be lambs and other young animals. You should hope there'll be sheepdog pups too, because they are soft and very cuddly, and will melt even the hardest heart.

My wife and I took our two grandsons here, and in a pen, we saw what was either a sheep or a goat - we're not sure which. Neither was the three-year-old, who after studying it puzzledly for a while, pointed to it and asked, "Can I have some food for that?". Maybe you'll be able to work out what "that" is. It could be a genetically-modified hybrid, in which case it'll be a shoat ..... or perhaps a geep.... Whatever, it's got a smile on its face.

An added bonus is the sheepdog trials every Tuesday, Thursday and Sunday at 2.30 weather permitting, and yes, they've heard all the jokes about three of them being found guilty! It's amazing to see these working dogs in action, taking their orders by way of just a whistle or word command.

There's a tearoom and picnic area, too. Note that, being on a hillside, it's pretty unsuitable for pushchairs, and there is only limited disabled access.

HOW TO GET THERE

The Farm Park is at the south end of the island, well signposted on the road between Whiting Bay and Lagg. Buses go from Brodick, and will stop at the gate.

OPENING TIMES

End March-end September, 10-5.30
Sun-Fri. Closed Saturday

CHARGES

Adults ££, children £

521
Holy Isle
Isle of Arran
HQ: The Holy Island Project, Kagyu Samye Ling, Eskdalemuir,
Dumfriesshire DG13 0QL
Tel: 01387 373232 ext 28   Fax: 01387 373223
Holy Isle North end phone: 07932 036481 (noon-1pm or 6-7pm only).
South end: 07775 766671
Email: office@holyisland.org
Websites: www.samye.org   www.holyisland.org

You couldn't class Holy Isle as a Visitor Attraction in the accepted sense, but it is definitely a place worth visiting, so I've given it an entry to itself.

The island is privately owned by the Buddhist monks from the Samye Ling Monastery in Dumfriesshire. The Holy Isle monks live in the lighthouse buildings at the southern end, and use it as a place of retreat and contemplation. Accommodation is available for those who wish their own form of solitude. The island has been recognised as a Sacred Site by the Alliance for Religions and Conservation. Volunteers have renovated the old farmhouse at the western side, turning it into a multi-faith Retreat Centre, and around 27,000 indigenous Scottish trees have been planted, including *Sorbus Arranensis* and *Sorbus Rupicola*, 2 very rare Whitebeams, unique to Arran. Whitebeam is a variety of Rowan or Mountain Ash, and it is hoped in years to come to sell seeds and saplings commercially.

The island is called "Holy" because of its associations with St Molaise, an Irish monk who lived there as a hermit around 600 AD. There is a story that the saint died on Arran at the ripe, even over-ripe, old age of 129, but there are precious few facts to back it. Sitting bang in the middle of Lamlash Bay, the view of it coming down the hill into the village is fantastic at any time of the year.

A small boat runs ferry services to the island several times a day in summer from Lamlash, and visitors are welcome, though under certain conditions.

Fires, alcohol, litter, overnight stays, pets and smoking are all banned, but visitors are free to walk anywhere they choose. You may take a picnic, but you **must** take your litter home with you. A leaflet is published with ferry times and an explanation of the project, and it asks visitors to refrain from *"....killing, stealing, lying, taking intoxicants, and sexual misconduct...."*, so there you are, you're well warned.

The shore path on the west shoreline from the jetty opposite Lamlash to the lighthouse is very easy, and you'll pass the Saint's cave and his 'well'. (Actually, it's just a small pool, but the water's delicious. Oh, and DON'T throw money into it!) The shallow cave was where the saint lived a very frugal and simple life, and was once visited by author Lewis Carroll. Also seen along the path, are many colourful rock paintings of Buddhist gods, completed in recent years by some of the nuns.

The other way to the south end is by going over the top via the summit of 1030 feet (314 m). Obviously, this route is for the fitter, experienced walker, and great care must be taken on the steeper slopes. On either route, you may see some of the Eriskay horses, or Soay sheep and goats which live wild on the island, seabirds of all kinds, seals, dragonflies, even big hairy caterpillars!

It is known that, before the Battle of Largs in 1263 (see entries, 'Pencil Monument', and 'Vikingar!'), the Viking fleet anchored in the sheltered bay, and it must have been a magnificent, if terrifying, sight. Viking runes, which probably date from the same time, can be seen scratched on the Saint's cave wall. Their translation basically says, 'Nikolas was here', and 'Vigleikr was here'. It is known that Vigleikr was a commander in the Viking king's army, so he must have taken part in the battle.

During the last two World Wars, a large fleet of British and Allied ships anchored here too, and it was said that there were so many ships, it was possible to walk right across the bay.

Needless to say, there are no public toilets. Neither is there disabled access, as you get on and off the island from a small motor boat.

HOW TO GET THERE

The boat runs May-September weather permitting, between 10am and 5pm from the Old Pier, Lamlash.
The cost is approx. £7 return per adult/£4 per child, most of it going to the monks, but for the peace and solitude you'll get on the island, it's worth it

Arran - Other Things

There are many other things to do and see on Arran, some energetic, some not. Here are most of the best.
Get full details at the Tourist Information Centre at Brodick Pier.

Abernethy Trust:
Near the coast at Blackwaterfoot, they offer activities such as canoeing, gorge walking, hillwalking, cycling, etc.
Accommodation is available in 2 to 6-bed rooms. Tel 01770 860333 for details.

Ancient Monuments:
Man has been on Arran for thousands of years, and of course has left his mark. There are standing stones, stone circles, and burial cairns on many parts of the island. The most important ones are at **Machrie Moor,** the remains of six stone circles, and one of the most important sites of its type in the UK. It's an easy walk to them; **Auchagallon,** a burial cairn and stone circle; **Moss Farm Road,** a cairn and stone circle; **Torrylin Cairn,** a chambered cairn; **Carnban,** a famous Neolithic "long" cairn; and **Torr A'Chaisteal Fort,** an Iron Age fort site.
Full information is available at the Tourist Information Centre.

Bike Hire:
Mini Golf Cycle Hire at the mini golf area, Brodick seafront; **Brodick Cycles** opposite the village hall; **Brodick Boat and Cycle Hire** at the beach, and **Whiting Bay Hires** in Whiting Bay.
They all supply helmets, child carriers, etc. free, and they all require deposits.
Most hires start at around £5 per adult for two hours (mountain bike), £2 per child for two hours (single speed model). All have daily and weekly rates.

Boat Hire:
Brodick Boat & Cycle Hire is at the beach. Dinghies with engine, sailing dinghies, rowing boats, canoes, wind surfer and wet suit available. Life jackets supplied. Evening fishing July and August. Fishing rods and bait. Tel. 01770 302868 or 302009.
King's Cross Dinghy Sailing Tuition. Situated between Lamlash and Whiting Bay. Approx £7.50/hour, £20/half day per head. Max. 3 people. Tel. 01770 700442, pm only.
Johnston's Marine Hire, Lamlash at the Old Pier. Chandlery, waterproofs and footwear, charts and books for sale. All fishing supplies. Subaqua equipment for sale. Information on wrecks and shore dives. Tel. 01770 600333.
Lamlash Boat Hire, Old Pier. Self-drive boats. Mackerel fishing trips June-September. Rods, bait and qualified skipper available. 16ft boats for sea angling, rods and bait supplied. Phone Tom on 01770 600998, or Harold on 01770 600349, or visit the old caravan on the pier behind the lifeboat station.
Whiting Bay Hires. 14ft motor boats for 4. Life jackets, fishing rods and bait supplied. Evening hires July and August. Tel. 01770 700382.

Catacol:

Just past Lochranza, on the road to Blackwaterfoot, you'll pass through the blink-and-you'll-miss-it hamlet of Catacol, consisting mainly of a row of cottages known as the Twelve Apostles. They were built around 1860 by the ruling Hamilton family for inhabitants of an inland settlement who were being moved out to make room for deer and game, but the people refused to live in them. The houses are very picturesque, and are one of the most photographed parts of the island, though it's difficult to get a good angle that doesn't include the power line poles in front of them!

Corrie:

Speaking of "most photographed parts of the island", this village is one of the others. Here, the road narrows greatly, with the houses on one side, their gardens on the other.

This only lasts a few yards, but in those few yards, the locals in their whitewashed houses manage to grow a colourful and blinding variety of summer bedding plants, climbers and roses-round-the-door, leading to its photogenic qualities.

At the 'new' harbour, look out for the bollards in the shape of sheep. Also here, sits a large pile of sandstone blocks, abandoned in 1928 when the bottom fell out the island's sandstone exporting market. Must have been some crash. . . .

Fishing:

There is open fishing on four rivers, if there's been plenty rain (what do I mean "if"?). Salmon and sea trout fishing is on the west coast on the Machrie river. Fly and bait fishing is at Port-na-Lochan Fishery, Blackwaterfoot. Loch fishing is at Loch Garbad. Full information at the Tourist Information Centre.

Flying Fever:

It's not flying a plane, but Paragliding - you know, where you jump off a hill with just a few square yards of brightly-coloured nylon between you and a Ouija board. A team of highly qualified instructors will take beginners through their paces. Tandem flights, and

I'll resist the obvious joke, start at around £35. I'm told it's a fantastic experience, but being a highly qualified 'feartie', I wouldn't know. Phone 01770 820292 for details.

Golf:
Arran is extremely popular with golfers. There are seven courses on the island, at **Brodick,** tel. 01770 302349, **Corrie,** 9 holes, at Sannox, tel. 01770 810223, **Lamlash,** tel. 01770 600296, **Lochranza,** tel. 01770 830273, and where an accepted hazard is deer strolling around on the fairways, **Machrie,** 9 holes, tel. 01770 850232, **Shiskine,** 12 holes, at Blackwaterfoot, tel 01770 860226, and **Whiting Bay**, tel. 01770 700487. Daily green fees go from around £8 to around £18 per adult. Some, like Lamlash and Whiting Bay have electric buggies for hire, booking in advance, and when you see the courses, you'll be grateful!

Pony Trekking:
Available at three centres, **Brodick Riding Centre,** tel. 01770 302800, **Cairnhouse Riding Centre** in Blackwaterfoot, tel. 01770 860466, and **North Sannox Pony Trekking Centre** at Sannox, tel.01770 810222, who also do short donkey & pony rides for youngsters. First-timers or experienced riders are welcome. All rides have qualified staff along and hard hats are supplied. Note - weight limits may apply.

Views:
There are many great views on Arran, of course, especially if you're an eagle or a mountain goat, but for the ordinary holidaymaker, the following four are exceptional:
♦ At the top of the hill on the road between Brodick and Lamlash is a small car park. Pull in, and there are picnic tables and a plaque showing the mountains and their names.
♦ The road up the glen between Sannox and Lochranza is known as the Bouguillie (colloquially pronounced 'Boogly'). At the bottom of the glen just before the road starts to climb, there's a big car park, where you can sit next to a roaring mountain stream of cold, peaty water, and from where hill walkers often start their journeys into the mountains. At the top of the glen, there's a layby where you should stop and look back. Not only will you get great views down the glen to the Cumbrae Isles and over to the Ayrshire coast, but it's a great place to see the mountains close up.
♦ The road over the hills from Brodick to Blackwaterfoot is known as the String Road. At its crest, stop and look back for more great panoramic views. To the right is the hillside used for hang-gliding, and in season, you'll often see the mad fools - sorry, thrill seekers - launching themselves into space.
♦ The road across the hills from Lamlash to the south end is the Ross road. It's uphill, twisty and through pine trees for most of the way, but at the summit it opens, and looking back, you'll get a great view of Holy Isle sitting spectacularly in Lamlash Bay. Beyond, you'll see most of the Ayrshire coastline. A little further on, you'll be rewarded by a super view of the long glen of the Sliddery Water sweeping down to the sea.

Walks:
Arran is synonymous with walking and climbing, some easy for any member of the family, and some only for the experienced climber, indeed, it is said that the northern mountains offer some of the best ridge walking in Europe. Goat Fell is an obvious choice, and can be 'bagged' by any fit person (unlike me), but please don't drag small children up there. People do go up in T-shirts, shorts and trainers, but you're heavily

advised not to, as the weather can change dramatically, even in Summer. The TIC will advise on the best walks, or there is a wide selection of books written by enthusiasts, and available anywhere they sell books. A good walk, which even I've done, is the Glenashdale Falls walk from Whiting Bay. At the top, and after a wet spell, you'll be rewarded with a spectacular 30-foot waterfall. If you want to cheat like I did, you can drive halfway up to the small car park. Just follow the signs from the main road in the town.

Wildlife:

You can't be on Arran and not see wildlife: indeed, you can be bitten by gnat-sized versions of it all over the island! If you're a lifelong townie, or from overseas, or just generally unfamiliar with the British countryside, you're in for a pleasant surprise. The Rangers at the Castle organise daily nature walks in the woods and on the shore. Evening walks are popular, but you MUST NOT forget your bug spray! All you have to do though, is travel around and keep your eyes and ears open, and you're bound to see or hear something.

Seabirds can be seen at any shore location of course, for instance at and around Corrie, north of the Castle. Cormorants and shags sit on the rocks drying their wings and having what I call Committee Meetings. Herons are plentiful, and will occasionally fly lazily across the road in front of you, looking for all the world like pterodactyls, or will be seen standing still at the water's edge. Owls will be heard at night, and pipistrelle and long-eared bats can be seen fleetingly at dusk. Buzzards, merlins, and falcons are pretty common, and can often be seen sitting on fenceposts or poles at the side of the road, quite unconcerned at passing traffic. Golden eagles can be spotted in the northern mountains if you're lucky, swirling lazily in the sky. There are many other types of birds of course, and the ornithologist will be spoiled for choice.

A good place to see seals is at Blackwaterfoot on the beach behind the Kinloch Hotel, and on the northern Newton shore at Lochranza, but the best place, and where I have never failed to see them sunbathing on the rocks, flippers lifted out the water, is on the shore or in the water near the Castle gates, except at high tide of course. There are a couple of places you can pull off the road to see them a bit closer. As I say, I've never failed to see them, and at all times of the year, but if by some remote chance there are none, it's a temporary state. Come back a little later, and I guarantee they'll be there.

Deer are quite easy to see in the mountains of the north. As you go over the hill and down the glen towards Lochranza, slow down if the road's clear, and look on the skyline to the right. Eight times out of ten you will see stags and their harem, and occasionally a little Bambi grazing quietly. Binoculars will help.

Closer encounters are often possible, too. Travelling after dark one night, I came upon a big stag trotting casually along the road near Sannox, and have seen them grazing on the golf fairway opposite the Distillery in the middle of the day. In the autumn mating season, the stags can be heard 'rutting' in the hills, filthy beasts.

The native red squirrel can be seen (there are no grey), as well as stoats, mink, and small furry and spiny things of that sort. There are badgers, but they're more difficult to spot, being more nocturnal.

If you're up very early near Corrie, you may see otters. If you're walking in the hills in long grass or bracken, keep half an eye open for the adder, or viper, the UK's only poisonous snake. You'll recognise it by the black and white V-shaped pattern on its skin. They're very shy though, and the noise of your approach will almost always frighten them off. Being bitten by one is practically unheard of.

In the sea on calm days, minke whales and porpoises are sometimes seen, and the ferry Captain told me he once saw dolphins chasing a porpoise. As he said, "They may be cousins, but they don't get on!".

If you're very lucky, like I was in 1999, you may see a basking shark in July, August or early September. It was slowly swimming along, just 150 yards from the main road at Whiting Bay. They're the second biggest shark in the world, sometimes up to 45 feet (15 m) long, but being vegetarians, they only eat plankton.

If you ever get a good view of one on a flat sea, they can look pretty scary, gliding along just under the surface with their huge mouths wide open, dorsal fins breaking the surface.

Some years ago, one passed close to a friend of mine while he was fishing from a small boat, and as he said, he nearly shot himself (and that's a deliberate typing error!). They pose no threat though, and swimmers under supervision have been known to swim alongside them.

Above: Deer like this magnificent specimen often wander on to the fairways at Lochranza Golf Club.

116

The Isle of Bute
Websites: www.isle-of-bute.com
www.isle-of-bute.net
www.visitbute.com

The island of Bute sits at the top of the Firth of Clyde. Administratively, it is included with Argyll, as in 'Argyll & Bute Regional Council' or similar, but it is so easily accessible from Ayrshire, that I have included it in this volume.

Ferries do the 35-minute crossing all day, all year, from Wemyss Bay (pronounced "weems", from the Gaelic meaning cave), which is *just* north of the Ayrshire border, by about a couple of hundred yards.

Bute is smaller than Arran, about 15 miles (24 km) long, by about 5 miles (8 km) across. Strangely though, it doesn't have the 'feel' of an island like Arran or Cumbrae. The population is just over 7300, so that's possibly the reason.

When you're in north Bute, you're technically in the Scottish Highlands, because the 340 million-year-old fault line which divides the Highlands from the Lowlands bisects the island. The line is marked in the Esplanade Gardens in Rothesay, the island's 'capital', so it's possible to stand with one foot in the Highlands, the other in the Lowlands! Not quite as exotic as the Equator, but hey, this is Scotland! Speaking of warmer climes, that old faithful, the North Atlantic Drift, works its influence again here, so in sheltered parts, you will notice the New Zealand cabbage trees, similar to those on Arran and Cumbrae.

Man, and presumably Woman, and no doubt her mother, has been here since the dawn of History (well, five and a half thousand years anyway, but with her mother there, it'll certainly feel longer!), and the island is littered, if not polluted, with prehistoric stone circles, cairns, Iron Age forts, and other antiquities. A comprehensive guide to all the sites can be bought at the Bute Museum (See chapter 53d).

There are many churches and chapels on the island, built when Christianity came to this part of the world from Ireland in the 6th Century.

Bute has many Royal connections, and you know how important good connections are. Rothesay was declared a Royal Burgh in 1400 by King Robert III, great grandson of Robert the Bruce. 1998 was the 600th anniversary of the granting of the hereditary title, *Duke of Rothesay*, given by Robert III to his son David. The title has been passed on, and is held nowadays by Prince Charles. 1998 was also the 500th anniversary of the granting of the title *Captain and Keeper of Rothesay Castle* to Ninian, Sheriff of Bute and Arran, a title which is still held today by the Bute family, direct descendants of Robert the Bruce.

Speaking of Royal connections, the actor and film director Richard Attenborough (**Lord** Attenborough, of course) has had a home here for many years, and he does take some part in the life of the island, for instance, using his influence in fund-raising for the new Isle of Bute Discovery Centre (see chapter 53b).

Rothesay was the home of Lena Zavaroni, a talented but ultimately tragic young singer. She shot to fame whilst still a child, but died in 1999 due to an eating disorder.

In past years, farming and fishing were Bute's main industries, and whilst they are still important, tourism is now the island's biggest earner. Open-top buses go all over the island from the pier area.

Fortunately, the island is easy to get to and from. Not only is there the main ferry terminal at Rothesay, but there is another ferry in the north at Rhubodach. From here, it's a five-minute journey across the famous narrow sea passage of the Kyles of Bute to Colintraive, and on to the tourist honeypots of Argyll, the Trossachs and the Western Highlands. Colintraive comes from the Gaelic meaning 'the swimming strait' and refers to the times when crofters swam their cattle across the kyle, or strait, to the mainland markets.

If you have time, take this route and go around the top of Loch Riddon to the high-up viewpoint. On a clear day, you'll be rewarded with a jaw-dropping view looking right down the Kyles to Arran and beyond. It's easily one of the best views in Scotland, if not the whole of the UK. I don't have the words to describe it: go and see it for yourself, but choose a clear day.

The Isle of Bute Discovery Centre—see chapter 53B.

53a
Rothesay's Victorian Toilets
The Pier, Rothesay

I'm not kidding, they're a genuine, award-winning, visitor attraction on Rothesay's pier, if you'll pardon the pun. In fact, in Scotland, they're famous! They've even been featured on national TV, in a BBC series about Victorian architectural treasures.

When they were built in 1899, Bute was a highly popular destination with "doon the watter" holidaymakers from Glasgow, and the beer was thin and watery, hence their need.

In those days, it was Gents only, as the thought of ladies going to the loo "in public" as it were, was too much for Victorian modesty to countenance. They cost £530, an extraordinary amount of money, and were restored in 1994 at a cost of £300,000, an *unbelievable* amount of money. True, this included the building of a Ladies section, but it's not half as fab as the gents, or so I'm told.

This palatial 'Temple of Convenience' features bold ceramic tiles, mosaic floors, marble, enamel and polished copper by the shedload, and uniquely, glass cisterns. (They stop short of glass toilet bowls, though - the Victorians weren't <u>that</u> crazy!)

Maybe they had the same designer as Mount Stuart (see separate entry), but anyway, they're well worth going to see, and a souvenir photograph **of the exterior** will bring a smile to the folks back home.

A sign outside says, *"Visitors, especially female visitors, are offered the opportunity to view the Gents at the following times: 10am, 1pm, 4pm"*, and they mean the facilities, not the occupants.

The toilet's showers are available for use by visiting yachts, or rather, by the people who sail in them. There's a display of photographs taken during the restoration, so you've got something to look at while you're in there. At least, there is in the Gents.

(You have no idea how difficult it's been not to make jokes about this entry. I've really had to be careful to mind my P's and Q's!)

HOW TO GET THERE
They're on the pier (I've done that gag!), and are practically the first thing you see when you come off the ferry.

OPENING TIMES
Easter-October, 8-9,
November-March, 9-5.

CHARGES
Adults 10p, schoolchildren free!

53b
Isle of Bute Discovery Centre
Winter Gardens, Victoria Street, Rothesay PA20 0AH
Tel: 01700 502462 or 502487

This 'A' Listed building was added to an existing bandstand in 1924, and before the days of cheap Spanish package tours for the huddled masses, it was an important venue on the holiday resort circuit of seaside theatres right up to the 1960's.

Every popular Scottish entertainer played here, but eventually it fell into disuse and disrepair, as indeed, did most of the entertainers.

In the 1980's, it became the focus of an energetic and vociferous campaign, backed by entertainers, local businesses and public bodies of the time, to have it restored. Fortunately, the campaign was successful, and the refurbished circular iron structure with glass domed roof was reopened in 1990 as a multi-purpose venue for cinema, live entertainment and other events.

Now though, there has been a campaign for the 21st Century, and, thanks to around £600,000 of funding from several bodies, including the Lottery Fund, it was re-launched in September 2001 by well-known Scottish Entertainer Johnnie Beattie and Lord Richard Attenborough (who has a house on the island) as the Discovery Centre.

Inside are interactive computer display panels and flat-screen TVs showing the history, geology, flora and fauna of the island, and computers where you can look for your Bute ancestors. Apparently, natives of Bute are called Brandanes. Surely they should be called Butanes? Taking that logic further, since the Gaelic name for Scotland is Alba, we should be called Albanians!

Anyway, also in the Centre is the Discovery Theatre, where, on the small variety stage, an animatronic figure of Johnnie Beattie explains all about the well-known acts who appeared in Rothesay. Look him straight in the eye, behind his clear plastic mask, and he'll wink at you. I think it's creepy, but see what you think.

Adjacent, is the small cinema, where you can watch a free, but brilliant, eight-minute film of Bute's attractions. There is full disabled access.

HOW TO GET THERE

It sits on a prime site on the promenade, near the pier and attractive gardens and the putting green.

OPENING TIMES
All year, but precise times depend on what's on.

CHARGES
Free.
Separate charge for evening feature films.

53c
Rothesay Castle
Rothesay, Isle of Bute
Tel: 01700 502691

This was already a well-established castle when it was attacked by Vikings around 1230, being built on the site of earlier earthworks. They couldn't get over the 20 foot high walls (they were all under six foot), so they decided just to hack their way through with axes. That's the story anyway, but it may well be true, as they wrote about it in their Sagas, the Viking stories, not the over-50's tour companies. Their King, Haakon, thought to himself, in fluent Viking, "By my big beard, this is a nice place, I'll take it", and took up residence for a while, but he did a moonlight flit after his defeat at the Battle of Largs in 1263, when Alexander III said to himself, "By my new hat, this is a nice place, but that hideous Viking wallpaper'll have to go", and moved in instead. It fell into English hands during the Wars of Independence, but Robert the Bruce kicked them out in 1311. He said to himself, "By my big sword, this is a nice place, and it's on an island - I think I'll move the wife's mother in here". In the early 1500's, James IV and James V thought it a nice place, and stayed there quite often for their holidays. During the English Civil War, the Earl of Lennox captured it on behalf of King Charles, thinking, "By my silk breeches, the King'll think this is a nice place, and I'll be well in with him. I hope it doesn't go to his head, though". But it did. Cromwell kicked the Earl out, couldn't make up his mind whether it was a nice place or not due to a complete lack of a sense of humour, and partially dismantled it when he slammed the door on the way out in 1660. When a busload of the Duke of Argyll's football hooligans came to it in 1685, they thought, "By oor kilts, this is no' a very nice place, it's fallin' tae bits", and burnt what was left of it to the ground out of sheer badness and too much strong cider. Successive Marquesses of Bute thought, "Right, stop this, it's getting very silly", and repairs were started in the 18th Century. Now, it is in the care of Historic Scotland, and a good thing too.

The castle has many distinctive features. Although partially a ruin thanks to Cromwell, its tall circular walls, four huge round towers and deep moat with ducks are very impressive. The restored Great Hall measures about 50 feet by 25 feet (15 m by 7.5 m), and has a huge fireplace (a Great Grate!), and a room that size in a Scottish castle needed it, believe me. The upper floors have lavatory chutes which emptied directly into the moat, so I'll leave you to create your own picture of the consequences of that! The courtyard is unique in Scotland, being round. Behind the chapel is the Bloody Stair, if you'll pardon the expression, so called because a nobleman's daughter stabbed herself to death here, rather than go through with an arranged marriage to some haggard hairy highlander with halitosis.

More fun stories are available at the castle. Scottish Tourist Board Commended.

HOW TO GET THERE
The castle is right in the centre of the town, so you can't miss it. When you come off the ferry, go up the road directly in front of you, and it's on the right.

OPENING TIMES
Apr-Sept, 9.30-6.30, Mon-Sat. 2-6.30 Sunday.
Oct-March, 9.30-4.30, Mon-Sat. 2-4.30 Sunday, but closed Thursday afternoons and Fridays in winter.

CHARGES
£. Concessions.

121

53d
Bute Museum
Stuart Street, Rothesay
Tel: 01700 505067

Situated behind the castle, this is a small, but packed and interesting museum. The building was given to the town in 1926 by the fourth Marquess of Bute, specifically for museum and archival purposes. The island has many archivals, some large, some small, and this is the place they're kept.

There are two main sections - one has genuine artefacts and very informative displays from every period of the island's history, from Stone Age man to Clyde 'Puffers', small steam cargo vessels. If you've read 'Tales of Para Handy' by Neil Munro, you'll know all about Puffers and the characters who sailed in them. If not, learn about them here.

The other section has detailed descriptions of the island's geology, examples of its bird and animal life from seashore to hills, and in summer, a large display and descriptions of local wild flowers. For youngsters, there's a Touch Table and a small aquarium.

The museum is a recognised source of information on the social history of Bute too, and there is a collection of pictures and photographs of old Rothesay and other local areas.

Guided tours can be arranged, and the shop has a good selection of gifts, crafts, souvenirs, books, etc.

There is full disabled access and assistance available.

HOW TO GET THERE

Stuart Street is just off the town centre, directly behind the castle.

OPENING TIMES

Apr-Sept,
Mon-Sat, 10.30-4.30. Sundays 2.30-4.30.
Oct-March,
Tues-Sat 2.30-4.30. Sundays 2.30-4.30.

CHARGES

£, plus concessions

Ascog Hall Victorian Fernery & Gardens
Ascog, Isle of Bute, Argyll PA20 9EU
Tel: *01700 504555.*
Website: *www.york.ac.uk/depts/biol/units/ground/ascog/welcome.htm*
(Honest, it works!)

Ascog was very much a lost garden until 1986 (it probably got lost in its own web address!), when the present owners bought the crumbling house and overgrown grounds, and began an extensive restoration programme, with assistance from Historic Scotland and the Royal Botanic Gardens in Edinburgh.

Ferneries were very popular when it was built around 1879, but nothing much of the original planting remained. However, a few treasures were discovered, and the sunken fernery with its beautiful red sandstone walls and water pool emerged from under the neglect of many years. One fern, *Todea Barbara,* is about the only survivor from the original collection. It's only about 4 feet (1.5 m) high, but is believed to be around 1000 years old. Yes, I said **one thousand**!

The impressive iron-framed glasshouse has now been restored to its former glory, and is the only one of its kind in Scotland. Amongst pteridologists - fern lovers to you and me - it is classed as the Eighth Wonder of the World. With meticulous care and thought, a new collection of around eighty exotic sub-tropical ferns has been planted, and they create a fascinating picture of Victorian-style splendour. There are ferns from Australia, New Zealand, South America, China, Japan, Asia and the Atlantic islands. Be aware that, being a glasshouse, it's warm and wet.

Outside, a peaceful path winds through colourful beds of flowers and plants in the garden, and throughout the season, the ever-changing colours, scents and textures please the eye, stimulate the nostrils, and lower the blood pressure. The owners are very friendly, and Mr Fyfe will talk to you for hours about all sorts of things!

There are guided tours and disabled access.

NB - No dogs allowed.

HOW TO GET THERE

Ascog is approximately 3 miles (4.8 km) south of Rothesay on the A844. Buses run from town and will stop at the gates.

OPENING TIMES

Mid Apr-mid Oct, 10-5.
Closed Mondays and Tuesdays.

CHARGES

££. Supervised children free.

Mount Stuart House and Gardens

Isle of Bute, Argyll PA20 9LP
Tel: 01700 503877 Fax: 01700 505313
Email: contactus@mountstuart.com
Website: www.mountstuart.com

Many extravagant adjectives have been used to describe Mount Stuart - magnificent, spectacular, exotic, breathtaking - and all are correct. It's quite unlike any other stately home I've ever been in, and you will either love it or hate it. You will either rank it with some of the most beautiful houses in the world, or you will flee, screaming for your mother. How can I describe it? Well, let's put it this way - it's not the kind of place you want to be with a bad hangover or a blinding headache, and I mean that in the nicest way.

Most of the original house was destroyed by fire in 1877, so when the third Marquess of Bute came to rebuild, he decided to incorporate his obsessions of art, astrology and religion into the design. No expense was spared, as it was said he had an income of £300,000 per year and was the richest man in Britain. He engaged Scottish architect Robert Rowand Anderson, and together they came up with this incredible fantasy, one of the finest examples of the most completely outrageous Victorian Gothic architecture in Britain. You'll think they were either geniuses or madmen, or 'on' something - maybe all three.

There is marble, gold leaf, brass, copper, colour and stained glass everywhere. The windows high up in the enormous square Reception Hall represent the signs of the Zodiac, and when the sun shines through them, it creates an incredible psychedelic rainbow of light and colour. Like, wow man!

The Horoscope Bedroom has a ceiling which is similarly decorated, with marble pillars and Gothic arches, and it even has its own conservatory off. In the Chapel is a high dome, called a lantern, and its stained glass windows are blood red, a very strange effect, very Russian. Everything is in perfect condition, and it looks as if it was finished just yesterday, a tribute I suppose, to the army of domestic servants there must have been.

When completed, it was the first house in Scotland to be lit by electricity, although I have to say the same claim has been made by Netherhall House in Largs, erected in 1875. Since its builder was Lord Kelvin, the famous Scottish scientist (OK, he was born in Belfast!) who made advances in electricity, navigation and thermodynamics, and after whom the Kelvin scale of temperature measurement is named, perhaps it has the edge by a couple of years. However, Mount Stuart got its first telephone only a year after the infernal machine's invention, and it claims to have been the first house **in Britain** to have its own indoor heated swimming pool!

As the history of the family goes back many hundreds of years, there is a fine collection of large portraits of long-deceased Butes.

The gardens are well worth seeing, too, and create a haven of normality after the excesses of the house. In the large glass pavilion in the grounds, a controlled microclimate has been created to support mountain and rainforest plant specimens from around the world.

Nearby is the Victorian Pinetum of North American conifers, and the new Arboretum is divided into sections representing major regions of the world. This latter display is part of the International Conifer Conservation Project by the Royal Botanic Gardens, Edinburgh, and try saying that lot after a few drinks!

A famous limetree avenue leads the visitor gently to the beautiful sandy shore (wasn't she was a singer in the 60's?), where picnics can be enjoyed, and where your vision can return to normal. Incidentally, the present Marquess is Johnny Dumfries, the ex-Formula One racing driver. He now likes to be called Johnny Bute, which gives a whole new meaning to these "I Love Bute" bumper stickers!

There is a new visitor centre with souvenir and gift shop, restaurant, audio-visual theatre and gallery, courtesy shuttle carriage to the House, guided tours, explanatory displays, loop system for the deaf, adventure playground, and picnic areas, and 300 acres (120 ha) of grounds, gardens and woodlands.

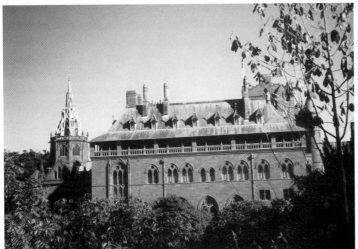

A beautiful place. You can easily spend the whole day here.

There is full disabled access and guide dogs are welcome.

Scottish Tourist Board Highly Commended.

HOW TO GET THERE

Leave Rothesay on the A844 south. Mount Stuart is about 5 miles (8 km) along the road.

Buses run from town.

OPENING TIMES

Weekends only, April & October.
Easter weekend, then May-end Sept 5 days, closed Tuesdays and Thursdays.
House 11-5. Gardens 10-6.
Pre-booked guided House, Gardens and Ranger tours available.
Winter access by arrangement.

CHARGES

House & Gardens:
££££ adults, ££ children. £££££ families. Concessions.
Gardens only:
£££ adults, ££ children, £££ families. Concessions.

Special Day Return Ticket from Glasgow Central and manned Strathclyde stations -
approx £16, kids £8 including train, ferry, bus and admission.
(This is a very good deal!)

53g
Ardencraig Gardens & Aviary
Ardencraig Lane, Rothesay PA20 9EZ
Tel: 01700 504644

The gardens were originally laid out for the owners of Ardencraig House around 1920, and were acquired by the local Council in 1970. They now house the working greenhouses and show garden which produce all the display flowers used in Rothesay.

Through development over the years, they now have a fine collection of rare and new plants, a Cactus House containing hundreds of varieties of cacti and succulents, and where you'll see some very odd-looking specimens, greenhouses with a blinding display of scores of plants of every shade of every colour of the rainbow, and not a greenfly in sight. They are the perfect example of how to grow flowering plants, given the right conditions.

The aviary in the garden is a fairly new venture, with many foreign species, including the West African Violacious Touracou (I kid you not!), unusual, beautiful, but very nervous! Running through the garden are two small trickling streams, ending in an ornamental fish pond.

During the season, there are some plants for sale, and their colours and scents will knock you out.

HOW TO GET THERE
From Rothesay, head towards Mount Stuart House.
On the left, sitting on its own on the shore, is the Craigmore Tearoom.
Turn first right after that into Albany Road.
At the junction, turn left, and look for the sign on the left.

OPENING TIMES

May-Sept,
9-4.30, Mon-Fri.
1-4.30, Saturday & Sunday.

CHARGES

Free, but you may spend
a fortune on plants!

The Creamery:
Bute cheese is well-known and very tasty. On a visit here, you can view the cheesemaking process in the factory, while an audio-visual presentation explains all the details. You'll be peckish after this, so there's a shop where you can sample the different cheeses and buy your favourites. Open May-August, 11-3pm.

Canada Hill, Rothesay:
It's a good walk up The Serpentine, a well-named twisting road reminiscent of the famous Lombard Street in San Francisco. The hill is so named because in days gone by, Bute residents would stand here to watch the ships passing on the Clyde, ships that were carrying their friends and relatives to a new life in North America. If you like, you can continue the walk to Ardencraig Gardens (see separate entry).

Ettrick Bay:
Ettrick Bay on the west coast has an attractive, mile-long white sand beach. There's an interesting walk of about 3 miles (4.8 km) north to the ruin of Kilmichael Chapel. On certain days, you'll get a good view of the famous paddle steamer *Waverley*, the last sea-going paddle steamer in the world, as she chugs her way round the Kyles to or from Tighnabruaich, a regular stop on the mainland. (See appendix) Take the B875 or the bus from town. Park here to climb Windy Hill, 912 ft (278 m).

Kames Castle:
Near Port Bannatyne, this is a massive tower house with walls 6 ft (2 m) thick, built in the 16th Century on earlier foundations. Here lived the Bannatynes of Kames, the right-hand men of the Stewart kings. The last of them died in 1790, but a nephew, Lord Kames, became a founder of the Bannatyne Club, important publishers of Scottish history and literature. He died penniless in 1833, and since then, the estate has been in private hands, so the castle is not open to the public. In the grounds of the estate is a restored and tiny fortified house. It measures only 25 ft by 21 ft (7.5 m by 6.5 m), and its story is an interesting one. In the 14th Century, the lands belonged to a family called McKinlay, and in an archery contest, the three sons beat the best of King's archers. But the Royal team were very bad losers, and unsportingly, set out to sort out their rivals. The McKinlay boys were so skilled though, that they killed a couple of dozen of them from a distance. This time, the King was really annoyed, and in revenge, he took the lands away from the McKinlays and gave them to his butler, or *dispenser*. The butler's descendants took the name Spens, and the family remained powerful and important for over three hundred years.

Kerrycroy:
Kerrycroy is a small, peaceful village on a sandy bay south of Rothesay, just before Mount Stuart House, and is a bit of an oddity. It was designed by Maria, the wife of the 2nd Marquess of Bute, and was modelled on what she thought a 'typical' English village looked like - timbered houses, small cottages and roses-round-the-door. Oh, well.

Kilchattan Bay (Locally pronounced Kil-*Cattan*):
The bay is south of Rothesay, and is a great place for picnics and chilling out on sunny days. There's a good sandy beach, or you can explore the interesting paths round the ruins of Kelspoke Castle and the lighthouse at Glencallum Bay. At the beginning of the 19th Century, there was a settlement of about fifty or so cottages here. It sounds remote and quiet, but the parish population of around 800 had three schools, a tileworks and six pubs to keep them busy! At the south end of the village is the comically-named Hawk's Neb Point, where fossils of fish have been dated to 200 million years old.

Kingarth:
Near this village south of Rothesay, is a Bronze Age circle of standing stones, an Iron Age fort, and early Christian monastic remains dedicated to St Blane, a 6th Century native of Bute. (See St Blane's Chapel.)

The Meadows Walk:
This walk takes you along High Street to the north end of Loch Fad. At the dam, there's a hide where you can watch the island's freshwater bird life. Something like 150 species have been recorded, and there are more ducks and geese than you can shake a feather duster at.
In summer, some of the rarer migrants to the UK are regular visitors, and hawks and other birds of prey can be seen in the hills. The island's shorelines are covered in oystercatchers, ducks, cormorants, and all kinds of feathery, flapping things.

Port Bannatyne:
At the end of the 19th Century, this village was a busy port for Clyde Puffers and passenger steamers. During the last War, midget submarines trained here, before setting off to engage the giant German battleship *Tirpitz.*

St Blane's Chapel:
The church is the ruins of a 12th Century chapel, but there is archaeological evidence of much earlier buildings. It is possible that this was a religious site long before even St Blane's time. He was born on Bute in the 6th Century, and was educated in Ireland, but returned and established the church here around 574 AD.
The medieval churchyard is in two sections, the upper section for the men, and the lower one for women.

This site is one of the most attractive places on the island.
It is in the south, 8 miles (13 km) from Rothesay on the A844, and ten minutes' easy walk from the car park at Kilchattan. In the care of Historic Scotland, there are many information boards and plaques. Access is free at all reasonable times.
A stone circle near the chapel is so old, it's prehistoric, and is known as 'The Devil's Cauldron'.

St Mary's Chapel:
This ruin is in the grounds of Rothesay's High Kirk, and was designated a Cathedral of the Isles in the 17th Century. It has many tombs, including those of some of the Marquesses of Bute. One tomb is reckoned to be that of Marjorie, Robert the Bruce's daughter, another possibly the tomb of King Robert II or maybe his father, Walter the Steward, in which case, it's extremely important.
Also here are the tombs of a 14th Century knight and his lady, and Stephanie, a relative of Napoleon. Quite what she's doing here, I don't know. Access is free at all reasonable times.

Scalpsie Bay:

This is about the best place to see seals. There's a car park and a viewing point. Get to it round the south of the island from Rothesay, or take the B878 west from town.

Sports:

The flat roads and light traffic make **cycling** an enjoyable and safe pastime. The Mountain Bike Centre will hire you everything you need, including tandems and trailers, and will also advise on the best hill routes. Phone 01700 502333.

Fly and coarse **fishing** of all types is available on Loch Fad, Quien Loch, Greenan Loch and Loch Ascog, where you might even hook a pike. Phone 01700 504871 for details.

Golf is available over 18 holes at Rothesay, tel. 01700 502244; 13 holes at Port Bannatyne, tel. 01700 504544; or 9 holes at Kingarth.

Pony trekking is ideally suited to Bute's quiet roads, woodland paths and sandy beaches, and there are centres for riders of all abilities at Kingarth, tel. 01700 831295, or at Rothesay Riding Centre, tel. 01700 504971.

Sailing in the Firth of Clyde is world famous and great fun, and Rothesay is a favourite port of call for boats from all over the UK and abroad. Prestigious sailing events are based here most years. Five-day RYA courses for all levels are available. Phone the Sailing School on 01700 502819, or Bute Berthing on 01700 500630.

Swimming can be done on many beaches or in Rothesay's Leisure Pool in the High Street, with sauna, fitness suite and solarium on the side. Kids Funtime is held on weekdays. Phone 01700 504300. Elsewhere, you can spend your day playing **tennis, putting, bowling, badminton, table tennis** and **snooker.**

Watersports of all types are well catered for on Bute, whether it's dinghy sailing, windsurfing or skiing. If you bring your own equipment, you can use the slipways in Rothesay Bay. Conditions are good all year for diving, especially round the Ascog area.

Straad:

It can be reached along the B878 west of Rothesay, via Ballanlay. Park in the village and explore the sand and shell beach. There are views over to the small island of Inchmarnock, and further to Arran and the Mull of Kintyre. At the north end of the beach is a ruined chapel, dedicated to St Ninian, another Irish missionary.

Walks:

There are many walks, some easy, some needing a bit more effort. Full information is available from the Rangers at Mount Stuart, or the Tourist Information Centre. The Island Discovery Tour is especially popular.

Public transport is limited, so you will need a car for some of the more inaccessible locations.

More information is available from the Isle of Bute Tourist Association on 01700 502151.

54
The Isle of Cumbrae
Websites: www.isle-of-cumbrae.net
www.largsuk.freeserve.co.uk/cumbrae.htm
or link from www.cimbrae.freeserve.co.uk
(No, that's not a typing error: it is CIMBRAE)

Cumbrae has a population of about 1400 on its 2,800 acres (1160 Ha), making it one of Scotland's most densely populated islands. It's only seven minutes (or about £15 per car in real money) from Largs, and in the summer, the small ferry runs every fifteen minutes from about 7 in the morning 'til about 8 at night. Buy your tickets before you board, or you'll cause terrible problems and hold-ups. Buses meet the ferries if you want to leave the car on the mainland.

Talking about prices, one wit has suggested that, mile for mile, travelling to Cumbrae is many hundreds of times more expensive than flying by Concorde, but I still think it's worth visiting. The first thing you'll see when you come off the ferry is a giant sandstone statue of a nun and a Viking, which sounds like the beginning of a bad joke - "There was a nun and a Viking walked into a bar....." - but they represent the island's religious and Viking heritage. Some islanders think it's an eyesore, stating that the money would have been spent better on improvements on the island, like restoring the town's pier, but others like it.

The first recorded mention of Cumbrae dates from 564 AD, when it was known as the 'Isle of Virgins'. This referred to the fact that a Celtic nun, St Maura, built a hospice on the island. Presumably, there were other nuns to help her, hence the title.

The adjacent island of Little Cumbrae is privately owned, and is now uninhabited. Here, lived another nun, St. Veya or Beya (there is a ruined chapel). In the 14th Century, it had a castle used by King Robert III, but Cromwell's troops (them again!) sacked it in 1653, seven years before they tried the same trick at Rothesay Castle further up the Clyde (see separate entry). At the time of writing, the island is for sale for a mere £2 million.

Cumbrae, from the Gaelic for shelter or refuge, is only about 10 miles (16 km) in circumference, and was a popular destination for "doon the watter" holidaymakers from Glasgow and other Scottish cities for many decades, as indeed was Bute and many Ayrshire resorts.
It's a nice place to visit, either for a day, or for a quiet, relaxing residency in one of its guest houses, hotels or holiday flats. As well as the small museum, aquarium and watersports centre mentioned below, the only town, Millport, has friendly cafes, bars, and shops, and there is an 18-hole golf course, riding stables, pitch & putt, tennis courts, crazy golf, hire bikes, and two fine sandy beaches to keep you occupied for a while. There is another good beach and tearoom at Fintry bay on the west coast.

Millport, or to be precise 50 Stuart Street along the seafront near the town centre, is the location of The Wedge, listed in the Guinness Book of Records as the narrowest

130

house in the UK. How narrow? 47 inches (119 cm), that's how narrow!

A good walk or drive on the island is the 'Inner Circle', a circular route from the town to the Glaid Stone. This is the highest point on the island at 417 feet (127 metres), and from here you will get exceptional panoramic views. On a good day, you will see Ben Lomond to the north, the Paps of Jura to the west, and Ailsa Craig and maybe even the coast of Ireland to the south.

Wildlife abounds on Cumbrae. On and near the coasts are birds of all types, from gulls to oystercatchers to eider ducks to geese to plovers, even tree creepers and, the name that's on everyone's lips, the bartailed godwit ! Inland can be seen buzzards, kestrels and sparrowhawks, and they eat some of the rabbits, mice, voles and lizards which live here. The island is particularly blessed with many varieties of wild flowers. Eight or nine species of orchid can be found, as well as many types of moor and marshland plants.

Two events on Cumbrae are worth a particular mention. At the end of August, Millport goes absolutely crazy when it stages a Country and Western Festival, with Civil War battle re-enactments, fast draw competitions, the inevitable line dancing, and more guitar-pluckin', horn-swogglin' bands singing more authentic Frontier gibberish than you can shake a rattlesnake at. It seems like everybody joins in and almost without exception, the shops erect false frontages to turn it into a Wild West town.

All the pubs change their names temporarily to things like Diamond Lil's Saloon, the café becomes Fort Apache, and the estate agent's becomes Pecos Pete's Land Agents. Even empty shops have their windows decorated, and the main street and boats in the harbour are bedecked with Old Glory and Confederate flags.

For all I know, they may even have spitting competitions and everyone eats beans! People come from all over the UK to this festival, and it's great fun, so I'm told. If you're into this, phone 01475 531106, shout "Yeeha!", and see where it gets you, or go to www.geocities.com/millportfestival.

At the holiday weekend at the end of September, things liven up again for The Illuminations. Local councils and businesses sponsor the event, practically every resident and shop puts special light displays in their windows, and there are strings of coloured lights along the seafront.

There is a prize for the best display, and on the Saturday night, there's a spectacular fireworks display which can be seen from many parts of the Ayrshire coast.

More information is available from the Tourist Information Centre opposite Millport Pier or phone the Isle of Cumbrae Tourist Association on 01475 530753.

54a
The Scottish National Watersports Centre
Isle of Cumbrae, Ayrshire KA28 0HQ
Phone: 01475 530757   Fax: 01475 530013

Courses in all types of water-based activities are on offer to suit all standards and abilities. You can learn how to sail anything from a kayak to a cruiser to a powerboat, either as skipper or crew member, or you can learn windsurfing or even marine diesel engine maintenance.

There are also junior courses for 9-14 year olds in dinghy sailing or windsurfing, novice or not. All courses can be residential in the Centre's own chalet accommodation with recently upgraded dining rooms, changing rooms and lecture rooms, and they have loads of modern boats and craft of all types. Cruises go as far as the Hebrides, and the Centre is hoping to start winter cruises abroad. The tutors are all friendly, enthusiastic and highly qualified.

If you or your kids are into boats, or you would like to be, this would be an ideal place to spend part of the summer. An information-packed brochure is available on request.

Note - they don't do fishing cruises or boat hire!

A view of Little Cumbrae with the snow-covered peaks of Arran in the distance.

HOW TO GET THERE

Turn left off the ferry towards Millport, and it's only a few hundred yards along the road on the right.

OPENING TIMES

Depending on activity. Phone for details.

CHARGES

Variable, depending on activity. Phone for details.

132

Robertson Museum & Aquarium
University Marine Biological Station, Millport,
Isle of Cumbrae KA28 0EG
Tel: 01475 530581 Fax: 01465 530601
Email: rupert.ormond@millport.gla.ac.uk
Website link from: www.northayrshiremuseums.org.uk

This scientific research and teaching establishment opened in 1897, and is now jointly operated and funded by several British universities. There is a small and interesting museum, dedicated in part to the work of David Robertson, a self-taught naturalist who came to work on the island. It was built due to his enthusiasm and painstaking research into the varied and rich life of the Clyde waters, and the work he started continues today. There are possessions and research materials which belonged to him, and a recreation of part of his original research facility, a floating laboratory called *The Ark.* In 2001, the museum was granted further funding which will not only ensure its continuation and restoration, but will also allow a new vessel to be built to carry on the research work into marine habitats and the management of national fish stocks.

Elsewhere in the museum are panels explaining the work of marine biologists in the conservation and physiology of the sea's flora and fauna. There is even a panel explaining how seaweed is made into products such as beer, shampoo, cheesecake, toothpaste and even ice cream - honest! There is also a small but excellent aquarium, and the tanks contain fish and shellfish of all types, all caught in local waters. No sharks, though. Children can handle crabs and yukky things like that, as can adults if they're brave enough. One-week holiday courses in all aspects of marine life are available, with accommodation if required. Disabled access.

It stands near to Lion Rock, so called because its shape looks like a crouching lion. This is a natural rock wall, one of several volcanic 'dykes' on the island. Locals have painted faces on some of them, so elsewhere on the island, look out for the Indian Rock and the Crocodile Rock!

HOW TO GET THERE

Turn left off the ferry and head towards Millport.
After about 3 miles (4.8 km) as you approach the outskirts of the town, the Station is a red sandstone building on the right.

OPENING TIMES

Open all year,
Mon-Thurs, 9.30-12.15, 2-4.45.
Fridays, closed at 4.15.
Saturdays also from June-September,
10-12.15, 2-4.45.

CHARGES

Adults, OAP's, children £.
Children under 5, free.

54c
Museum of The Cumbraes
Garrison Craft Studios, Millport, Isle of Cumbrae KA28 0DG
Tel: 01475 531191
Email: namuseum@globalnet.co.uk
Website link from: northayrshiremuseums.org.uk

Garrison House, as the original home of the museum is known, started life around 1745 as the barracks for the crews of the Revenue (Customs & Excise) boats, but it has also seen service as a convalescent home during both World Wars, a hotel, and even a TB hospital!

Up until recently, this was the museum, but it was falling to bits, so they had to move out, and it became an unsightly boarded-up empty shell. Then vandals set fire to it, because they thought that would improve it.

One day, it will be the new museum, maybe even incorporating luxury flats, but plans are moving very, very slowly, and I'm told it'll be several years before even a projected opening date can be set.

The rebuilding is going to be funded partly by the local Council but at the moment they are, shall we say, not exactly flush.

Until the new place opens, the only 'Museum of the Cumbraes' in located temporarily in one small room, part of the Craft Studios in the grounds of Garrison House. When I visited, there was a number of market stalls and kiddies rides there too.

They are only able to display a small number of exhibits, the vast bulk of the collection being in storage. Shame.

They do well though, to give you a taste of the island's history and there are photographs, many items of interest, and explanatory panels.

There is disabled access, as long as you don't mind a gentle uphill approach.

HOW TO GET THERE

Garrison House is on the main street in the town. Access is through the arch from the street to the left of the building.

OPENING TIMES

April-September,
Thurs - Mon, 11-1 & 2-4.30.

CHARGES

Free

54d
The Cathedral of the Isles
Millport, Isle of Cumbrae, Ayrshire KA28 0HE
Tel: 01475 530353   Fax: 01475 530204
Email: tccumbrae@argyll.anglican.org
Website: www.sol.co.uk/s/sedati/parish8.htm

The Episcopal Cathedral of the Isles, a highlight that shouldn't be missed, is another record holder, having the smallest nave in Europe, if not the world, with seating for only 100. Commissioned by George Boyle, the 6th Earl of Glasgow, and designed in the Victorian Gothic style by William Butterfield in 1876, it's undoubtedly a minor masterpiece, with lots of incredible wildflower detail and colour between the beams on the ceiling.

This pretty church received £801,000 from the Heritage Lottery Fund in October 2001, so it will be repaired and restored to its original glory.

The Scottish Episcopal Church offers accommodation in the adjacent College, a place of retreat or study, or for quiet holidays in a Christian environment. It is also used for the preparation of religious and sacred music, and concerts are often given in the church.

At the beginning of the 19th Century the local minister used to lead prayers *"for the Great and Little Cumbrae and the adjacent islands of Great Britain and Ireland"*, cheeky devil.

The Viking and Nun Statue, Cumbrae. See chapter 54.

<table>
<tr><td>

HOW TO GET THERE

The church is off George Street, on a hill at the back of the town centre. Cars can enter the grounds of the college up a stony, bumpy road from George Street.

</td><td>

OPENING TIMES

Not sure what they might be officially, but I just turned up on a summer weekday, and it was open

CHARGES

Free, of course, but donations welcome

</td></tr>
</table>

Andy, My Brain Hurts
Or
The (Optional) Anti-Confusion Ancient History Chapter

You've probably noticed, and I hope you'll be bloomin' grateful for the fact, that throughout the book, I've tried to avoid too much boring history and names and dates, in other words, all the stuff you and I hated about history at school.

However, it strikes me that a thumbnail sketch of some of the historical characters and events mentioned in the book would be acceptable, in order that you might better understand a little of who was who and what they did, at least in relation to Ayrshire or Scotland. What follows then, is a quick history lesson, if you want it.

Alexander III (1241-1286).

He was generally reckoned to be a strong, effective ruler of great character, the kind of guy that a younger Charlton Heston might play. He was only 7 when he was crowned, and his pedigree was such that, at the ceremony, a Celtic priest (that's **K**eltic, not Seltic!) read aloud his entire family tree in Gaelic - full of impressive detail maybe, but pretty dull otherwise. He is remembered most for sorting out the Vikings once and for all. Many Scottish islands had been under Norwegian rule for generations, but he decided it was time the Vikings departed, and they can take their smorgasbord and white wood furniture with them.

The Viking King Haakon mounted an attack on (hey, I'm a poet!) Scotland in July 1263, and anchored off Arran (see chapter 52l 'Holy Isle'), ready to resolve the situation with big axes. Smart Alexander, realising that Autumn gales were due soon, used all sorts of dodges and delaying tactics to waste time until the gales arrived. How and why experienced and sophisticated sailors like the Vikings fell for that old trick, we will never know. So the gales duly blew in September, just like today, driving many Viking ships aground near Largs (see chapter 11 'Pencil Monument'), creating dead Vikings, and causing consternation and confusion and wet feet. Haakon's forces withdrew in the huff, and just to complete their misery, Haakon died in Orkney on the way home.

To celebrate the new *entente cordiale*, Alexander allowed his daughter Margaret to marry King Eric II of Norway in 1281. The years that followed the signing of the Treaty were important for Scotland. Towns which traded with foreign ports prospered, agriculture and learning increased, and many great castles, abbeys and cathedrals were established.

The Wars of Independence.

Alexander III of Scotland may have been a great guy, but he fell off his horse and over a cliff edge in 1286. That didn't do him much harm, but it was the sudden stop at the bottom that killed him. His three-year-old granddaughter Margaret was named as successor, but unfortunately, the poor little lass died soon after the announcement, so the arguments started about who was next.

After lengthy discussion, John Balliol was crowned King, but Edward I of England expected Balliol to swear fealty to him. "Oh no I won't", said Balliol. "Oh yes you will", replied Edward in best Pantomime Villain fashion, and we can all guess at the outcome. This was the start of what became known as The Wars of Independence, Scottish conflicts with England which lasted three hundred years or so. Well, officially, that is, as some think they're still going on!

William Wallace, 1270-1305.

When he was 27, he killed the son of the English Sheriff of Lanark, possibly in revenge for the murder of his wife, or 'Murrrrn', as Mel Gibson called her. (This was a scene in 'Braveheart', but the location is all wrong, because there's too many jagged mountains for my liking. Still, that's Hollywood for you!)

Most Scots couldn't see much wrong with what Wallace did, as at the time, the English were strutting about as if they owned the place, and were, as we say here, 'acting it'. Actually, they would have said that they **did** own the place, since King Edward I had defeated the Scots forces at the Battle of Dunbar in 1296 and now ruled Scotland. (As punishment, he pinched our ancient Coronation Stone and took it to Westminster Abbey, and we didn't get it back until just recently.) Anyhow, this was the reason that Wallace was fighting for freedom, and after the killing of the Lanark Sheriff, many disgruntled individuals and clan chiefs from all over Scotland flocked to join Wallace to show solidarity, except noblemen, of course - they knew what side their bread was buttered on, and didn't want to risk upsetting Edward. Naturally, Edward sent an army to sort him out, but they were severely 'gubbed' at the Battle of Stirling Bridge, despite outnumbering the Scots. Wallace was hailed as the Peoples' Champion and was elected a Guardian of Scotland. Now, Edward was **really** upset, and Wallace was eventually betrayed, captured and 'tried' at Westminster.

The outcome was inevitable and terrible. He was hanged until he was only half dead, then disembowelled, then beheaded; the classic punishment of being hung, drawn and quartered. What you didn't see in the film was that his head was stuck on a spike on London Bridge, and his limbs were sent to various parts of the country to act as a warning to others, It was a not entirely successful warning, as it turned out.

King Robert I - Robert the Bruce, 1274-1329.

Was crowned in 1306. His father was Robert Bruce of Annandale, and his mother Marjorie, Countess of Carrick (southern Ayrshire). His daughter was also called Marjorie, and his grandson and great grandson were also called Robert - confusing, isn't it? Anyway, Robert THE Bruce was probably born at Turnberry Castle, which had a nice view and was very handy for the golf course. (The ruins of the castle are next to the lighthouse at the village of Maidens. The golf course doesn't advertise this fact, because you have to cross the course to get to them, and they don't like that, but alternatively, you can park near the Bruce Hotel in the village and walk along the shore).

At first, he sided with Edward like his father had, but later joined forces with Wallace declaring, "I have to be with my own", not "I vant to be alone" as has been misreported. When Edward proposed a truce, he re-sided with the English King, but during an argument at Dumfries with John Comyn, another Guardian of Scotland, Bruce murdered him. Again, and finally, he sided with Scotland, amid cries of "For God's sake, make up your mind!".

Many battles later, he faced the army of Edward II at the Battle of Bannockburn in 1314, and where, incidentally, he had 2000 Ayrshire men under his personal command. This famous battle ended in supreme victory for the Scots, ensured Bruce's place as one of Scotland's heroes, and kick-started the tourist industry in the Stirling area. Bruce's daughter Marjorie married Walter the Steward, hence the name Stewart, thereby beginning the line of Stewart monarchs. Bruce died of leprosy in 1329.

His heart was put in a casket to be taken by Sir James Douglas for burial in Jerusalem, but during a battle against the Saracens, Sir James threw the casket into the melee with the cry, "Go before, brave heart (ah-HA!), and I shall follow you or die!", which he did. The heart was retrieved and returned to Scotland, and was buried in Melrose Abbey in the Borders, where, in its recently-restored casket, it remains to this day.

King Robert II, 1316-1390.
Marjorie and Walter's son, and grandson of The Bruce, was crowned at the age of 54, but was not a very effective King, and didn't really want the job anyway. He ruled a land where, when not fighting the English, the clans were fighting each other!

Other minor irritations like the Black Plague, civil unrest and the Revolting Peasants in England took all the fun out of the job. To cheer himself up, he rebuilt Dundonald Castle (see separate entry), and stayed there quite a lot to get away from it all.

After twenty miserable years on the throne, he died at the castle at the age of 74, and was probably glad to get some peace.

King Robert III, 1337-1406.
Great grandson of The Bruce. He had been christened John, but it was not a popular name, due to several previous Johns being complete wastes of space.

When crowned at the age of 53, he took the name Robert. Just to confuse things even further, he had a brother also called Robert, but he was never King! By all accounts, was a gentle and sad man, but not physically fit enough for the rigours of monarchy due to an old riding accident, so he probably limped and spoke in a high voice as well.

He created the title Duke of Rothesay, held today by Prince Charles. Fearing for the safety of his 11-year-old son James (who became James I of Scotland), he sent him to France, but the ship was captured by English pirates, and the lad was 'obliged' to remain at the English Court for eighteen years.

News of his son's capture and house arrest probably contributed to his death, also at Dundonald like his father. He had already chosen his own epitaph - *"Here lies the worst of Kings and the most miserable of men in the whole realm".* Aw, bless. He hated his life so much that he had decreed he wanted to be buried in a rubbish heap, but it was decided that Paisley Abbey was more fitting.

James IV (1473-1513).

He is credited with subduing the belligerent clans of the Gaelic-speaking Western Isles, and bringing them under wholly Scottish rule. He was a patron of the Arts of the age, and was responsible for at least some of the construction of the fabulous palaces of Falkland, Linlithgow, Stirling Castle, King's College Aberdeen, and arguably the best-known of all, Holyrood Palace in Edinburgh. Perhaps for love, but certainly for political reasons, he married Margaret Tudor, daughter of Henry VII, thereby cooling English hostility a bit, and ensuring Stewart blood in the English Court. His major cockup though, was the Battle of Flodden.

During the uneasy peace that had followed his marriage, England had turned its aggression on France. France called in some old favours from James, and, caught up in the fervour of the moment, he led an army with some success in Ireland and northern England, and thought he could now take on all-comers. The disaster that was Flodden occurred on Sept 9th, 1513, when his force of around 10,000 men was beaten by the less well-equipped English army. The battle took with it not only the King, but the best of the Scottish knights. The event is commemorated in a heart-wrenching traditional song, 'The Flowers O' The Forest'.

James V (1512-1542).

James became King after his father's death at the Battle of Flodden. By all accounts, he was a cruel man, spending money like it was going out of fashion, and causing Scots to live in an almost permanent state of fear of arrest for the slightest reason.
This character trait is perhaps unsurprising, as his upbringing was not exactly smooth. He was only a year and a half old when he succeeded to the throne, and Court nobles fought and argued for years to control and influence him, first one way, then another. His mother, Margaret Tudor, changed her allegiance from the English to the French, so that sent out further confusing messages.

Popular gossip said that, when an adult, he wandered anonymously among the Great Unwashed in the guise of a beggar, leading to his Scots nickname of 'The Gaberlunzie Man'. He married Mary of Guise-Loraine in 1538, creating what became known as the Auld Alliance between Scotland and France, and which apparently is still technically in force today. Unsurprisingly, relations with England worsened. England was now ruled by Henry VIII, and he defeated James' forces at Solway Moss in 1542. In December that year, James' daughter, who became Mary Queen of Scots, was born, cheering everybody up a bit, but following his defeat in battle, he suffered a mental breakdown, and died on December 14, spoiling everyone's Christmas.

Oliver Cromwell (1599-1658).

The story of Cromwell is long and complicated, but basically (very!) it goes something like this: Cromwell was born into a strict Puritan family, which meant that they were fanatically religious, didn't find many things funny, and believed that everyone but them was going to burn in the fires of Hades. King Charles I had practically bankrupted England because he couldn't count very well, and he was also trying to force a new Prayer Book on Scotland, but we weren't too keen on it. Parliament refused to give Charles any more money, partly because he had barged his way into the Commons chamber demanding help. They didn't like that, or his links with Catholicism (yes, I'm afraid it all boils down to religious intolerance again!) Anyway, Civil War broke out, so Cromwell's New Model Army took over the running of the country, deciding to execute the King while they were at it. This didn't please the Monarchists, but Cromwell moved swiftly and ferociously to remove opposition, both in Scotland and in Ireland. Thus, areas where people were sympathetic to the idea of the return of a Stuart King in the person of Charles II, were put to the sword (see chapter 53c 'Rothesay Castle').

Cromwell was pronounced Lord Protector, and the Monarchy was restored after a fashion, but grudgingly, and with much less power. Upon Cromwell's death, his son Richard took up the job, but apparently, he was completely useless, and to everyone's relief, resigned shortly thereafter.

There are many, many books on Scottish history, some quite academic, some much less so, some even comical, so in any good book shop, you'll be spoiled for choice. An interesting book in my collection is "A Holiday History of Scotland" by Ronald Hamilton. It explains things fairly briefly and in words of one syllable, but it may be out of print. If that's not available, try "An Illustrated History of Scotland" by Elisabeth Fraser and published by Jarrold, or the "Pocket History of Scotland", published by Lomond Books. I got it for only £3 in a Tourist Information Centre.

Free Things

For anyone on a limited budget, here is an at-a-glance listing of all the free things to visit or to see, from those described in the book.

Many places will welcome donations, should you feel so inclined. Some you can spend half an hour at, some the whole day, so check each listing for details.

These should keep you going for a few days, so maybe the money you save can be used for one or more of the attractions that charge an entry fee. Again, it is in a roughly north to south listing.

Note - any National Trust for Scotland or Historic Scotland property has free entry if you're a member.

Ayrshire:
The Prophet's Grave, near Largs.
Largs Museum.
Skelmorlie Aisle, next to Largs Museum.
The Christian Heritage Museum, Largs.
Haylie Chambered Tomb, Douglas Park, Largs.
Haylie Brae picnic area, Largs.
Largs Yacht Haven.
The Pencil Monument, Largs.
Cornalees Bridge Visitor Centre, Loch Thom, Inverkip.
Lunderston Bay Picnic & Play Area, Gourock.
Castle Semple Water Park & Visitor Centre, Lochwinnoch.
RSPB Nature Centre, Lochwinnoch, visitor centre building.
Muirshiel Visitor Centre, Lochwinnoch.
Hunterston Power Station Visitor Centre, West Kilbride.
West Kilbride Museum, West Kilbride.
Portencross Castle (exterior)
Law Castle, West Kilbride (exterior)
North Ayrshire Museum, Saltcoats.
Kilwinning Abbey and Heritage Centre, Kilwinning.
Mother Lodge No. 0, Kilwinning.
Eglinton Country Park, Kilwinning.
Eglinton Castle, Eglinton Country Park.
Eglinton Trophy, Cunninghame House, Irvine.
Glasgow Vennel Museum & Gallery and Burns' Lodging House, Irvine
Irvine Burns Club & Burgh Museum, Irvine.
The Harbour Arts Centre, Irvine, gallery and bar events.
The Big Idea, Irvine Harbourside, restaurant and shop.
Pilot House, Irvine Harbour. (outside viewing only)
Beach Park, Irvine.
Dundonald Castle exterior.
Dick Institute, Kilmarnock.
Dean Castle Country Park, Kilmarnock.
Loudoun Castle Family Theme Park, Galston (free if you're under 0.9 metres tall!)

Kid'z Play, Prestwick (free for babies and adults accompanying paying children)
Pirate Pete's, Ayr (free for babies and adults accompanying paying children)
Craigie Horticultural & Visitor Centre, Ayr.
Ayrshire Archives Centre, Ayr.
Kirk Alloway, Monument & Gardens, Brig o' Doon, Alloway, Ayr.
Dunure Castle, The Electric Brae & Croy Shore, south of Ayr.
Cathcartston Visitor Centre, Dalmellington.
Loch Doon Castle, near Dalmellington.
Fishing on Loch Doon.
Bargany Gardens, by Girvan (donation appreciated).
Sawney Bean's Cave & Games Loup, near Ballantrae.
Robert Burns Centre, Dumfries.
Burns House, Dumfries.

Arran:

The Arran Ferry (free for under 5's)
Arran Aromatics Visitor Centre.
Isle of Arran Brewery (Free for kids)
Lochranza Castle.
King's Cave.
Balmichael Visitor Centre.
Arran views.
Arran walks.
Arran antiquities.

Bute:

The Rothesay Ferry (free for under 5's)
Rothesay's Victorian Toilets. (Well, only 10p for adults!)
Isle of Bute Discovery Centre.
Ardencraig Gardens & Aviary (Donation for upkeep of aviary appreciated).
Ascog Hall Victorian Fernery (Free for supervised children)
Bute views.
Bute walks.
Bute antiquities.

Cumbrae:

The Cumbrae Ferry (free for under 5's)
Robertson Museum and Aquarium (under 5's)
Museum of The Cumbraes.
The Cathedral of the Isles.
Cumbrae views.
Cumbrae walks.
Cumbrae antiquities.

You will also find some vouchers at the rear of this book
entitling you to even more free entries and special offers!

Appendix, spleen, pancreas and other juicy titbits . . . .

Ayrshire & Arran Tourist Board, Administration Centre
15a Skye Road, Prestwick KA9 2TA. Tel - 01292 678100. Fax 01292 471832.   Email - info@ayrshire-arran.com.
For day-to-day tourist information, see TIC address below.

Bus companies
For information on A1, AA, Stagecoach and Western bus services, call Ayr 01292 613500, Kilmarnock 01563 525192, Ardrossan 01294 607007 or Rothesay 01700 502076.
For enquiries about travel by Scottish City Link buses to and from major Scottish cities, call 0990 50 50 50.

Caledonian MacBrayne ferries
Ardrossan (for Arran) - Tel. 01294 463470.
Brodick, Isle of Arran - Tel. 01770 302166.
Wemyss Bay (for Bute) - Tel. 01475 520521.
Rothesay, Isle of Bute - Tel. 01700 502707.
Largs (for Cumbrae) - Tel. 01475 674134.

Caravanning (and camping)
Ayrshire, and indeed Scotland, is well served with caravan and camping sites, some small, some larger. Modern sites are well-equipped these days, most with power points, toilets, shops and laundry facilities. If you're touring, you'll probably have your own source of information about the various sites, otherwise, look for the web addresses below. There is one official Camping and Caravanning Club site, at Culzean Castle.
The Club's address is The Camping and Caravanning Club, Greenfields House, Westwood Way, Coventry CV4 8JH. Tel 02476 694995.
Website www.campingandcaravanningclub.co.uk

Disability Scotland
Information Dept., Princes House, 5 Shandwick Place, Edinburgh EH2 4RG.
Tel. 0131 229 8632. Alternatively, a leaflet, *Practical Information for Visitors with Disabilities,* is available from Tourist Board main offices.

Family Day Ticket
for up to 2 adults and 4 children or 1 adult and 2 children. Valid on trains, Glasgow Underground, some buses and even some ferries in the Strathclyde Passenger Transport area (basically the bottom left quarter of Scotland) for one day. Details at manned railway stations, Tourist Information Centres, and ticket issuing agencies.

Golf courses
Scotland is polluted with golf courses - there over 400 of them - and Ayrshire has many fine examples, some already mentioned. I'm not a golfer, but even I've

counted 44! Ayrshire is the only county in the UK with two Open Championship courses, Turnberry and Royal Troon, and is truly the home of the Open, being first staged at Prestwick in 1860.

There are public courses too, of course, run by local District Councils, and called Municipal courses. Green fees are generally a little cheaper than private courses.

Visitors are welcome except where mentioned.

In roughly north-south order, they are at:

Largs, Routenburn. Heathland - great views of the Firth of Clyde. Tel. 01475 687240.
Stevenston, Auchenharvie. Parkland/links, 9 holes. Tel. 01294 603103.
Irvine, Ravenspark. Parkland. No visitors Saturdays. Tel. 01294 276476.
Troon, Darley, Fullarton & Lochgreen. (3 courses in one location.) Tel. 01292 312578.
Kilmarnock, Annanhill. Parkland. Tel. 01563 521512.
Kilmarnock, Caprington. Parkland. Tel. 01563 521915.
Patna, Doon Valley. Moorland, 9 holes. Tel. 01292 531607.
Ayr, Belleisle. Parkland. Tel. 01292 441258.
(Ayr Belleisle is apparently the finest public course in Scotland.)
Ayr, Seafield. Parkland/links. Next to Belleisle. Tel. 01292 441258.
Ayr, Dalmilling. Meadowland. Tel. 01292 263893.
Maybole. Parkland, 9 holes. Tel. 01292 612000
Girvan. Parkland/links. Tel. 01465 714346.

Green fees and playing times vary bewilderingly, according to the course, the season, the day, maybe even the phases of the moon, for all I know. Phone for details!

A very good guide, *The Ayrshire & Arran Golf Guide*, is available free at most TIC's, and it will tell you everything about every course in the area.

Historic Scotland
Longmore House, Salisbury Place, Edinburgh EH9 1SH. Tel. 0131 668 8600.

Isle of Bute Jazz Festival
Held over the May Day Bank Holiday long weekend. Enquiries to 4 Ettrickdale Road, Port Bannatyne, Isle of Bute PA20 0QZ. Tel. 01700 502800, Fax. 01700 502860.

Leisure Centres
The best ones, other than those already mentioned. See also under 'Swimming Pools'.
Stevenston - Auchenharvie Leisure Centre, Saltcoats Road. Swimming, ice rink, gym. Tel. 01294 605126.
Kilmarnock - Galleon Leisure Centre, Titchfield Street. Swimming, ice rink, bowling, squash, games hall, creche. Tel. 01563 524014.
Kilmarnock - Hunter Leisure Centre, Ardbeg Avenue. Gym, sports hall. Tel. 01563 541350.
Darvel - Gavin Hamilton Sports Centre, Jamieson Road. Sports hall, gym. Tel. 01560 321949.
Galston - Loudoun Sports Centre, Newmilns Road. All-weather outdoor floodlit pitches, mini golf, pool & snooker. Tel. 01563 822061.
Prestwick - Centrum Arena, Ayr Road. Home to the Scottish Eagles, Scotland's only Super League Ice Hockey team. Skating rink, public sessions and lessons. Times vary. Tel. 01292 678822.
Ayr - Citadel Leisure Centre, South Harbour Street. Swimming, games hall, gym, spa. Tel. 01292 269793

National Trust for Scotland
Wemyss House, 28 Charlotte Square, Edinburgh, EH2 4ET.   Tel: 0131 243 9300. Fax: 0131 243 9301. Details can also be obtained from any of the Trust's properties, and depending of the time of year, you may get special deals on fees.

Paddle Steamer '*Waverley*'
Anderston Quay, Glasgow G3 8HA.   Tel: 0141 221 8152. Great fun. Day trips from many Clyde locations on the Last Sea-Going Paddle Steamer in the World. Close-up views of Arran and Ailsa Craig. See website addresses further on in this book.

Royal Society for the Protection of Birds
Unit 3/1, West of Scotland Science Park, Kelvin Campus, Glasgow G20 0SP. Tel. 0141 945 5224. Website - www.rspb.org

Scottish Tourist Board, now called Visit Scotland
23 Ravelston Terrace, Edinburgh EH4 3TP.   Brochure Hotline, 08705 511511; Enquiries, 0131 332 2433; Fax 0131 343 1513.

Swimming Pools
Other than those already mentioned. See also under 'Leisure Centres'.
There are also pools in:
Kilbirnie, Tel. 01505 683304;
Cumnock, a 1930's outdoor, heated pool, 01290 420803;
Prestwick, 01292 474015;
Troon, 01292 311758;
Maybole, 01655 882658;
Dalmellington, 01292 550665; and
Girvan, 01465 714545.

Ten-Pin Bowling
Saltcoats - Base Bowl, Hamilton Street. Tel. 01294 603801.
Kilmarnock - The Garage, Grange Street. Tel. 01563 573355. Also has karting.
Ayr - L.A. Bowl, Miller Road. Tel. 01292 611511.

Theatres
Borderline Theatre, North Harbour Street, Ayr. Converted church. Resident company and touring productions. Tel. 01292 281010.

Civic Theatre, Content Street, Ayr, opposite the fire station. A nice little theatre, sadly underused. Occasional local amateur companies and small touring productions. Tel. 01292 263755.

Gaiety Theatre,   Carrick Street, Ayr, just off the town centre. Nicely restored Victorian theatre, well-used, mainly touring variety and musical shows, occasional drama, summer variety season, Xmas panto. Tel. 01292 611222 or 264630.

Harbour Arts Centre, Harbour Street, Irvine. (See separate entry) Very intimate stage. Small touring productions, amateur drama, occasional concerts, lectures and festivals. Gallery. New bands Friday nights, 'Unplugged' and comedy sessions. Loads of classes for kids and all ages. Tel. 01294 274059.

Palace Theatre, Green Street, Kilmarnock, just off the town centre. Nice little theatre. Similar programme to Ayr's Gaiety. Xmas panto. Tel. 01563 537710 or 523590.

Tourist Information Centres
Ayr
22 Sandgate, south of the river, 150 yds uphill from the Town Hall. Tel 01292 290300.
Dumfries
64 Whitesands, on the riverside, next to the Coach & Horses pub. Tel. 01387 253862.
Girvan
(Seasonal) Bridge Street, just before the traffic lights in the centre of town. Tel/Fax. 01465 714950.
Irvine
New Street, opposite the railway station. Tel. 01294 313886. Fax 01294 313339. Email. irvine@ayrshire-arran.com
Isle of Arran
The Pier, Brodick, Isle of Arran. Tel. 01770 302140.   Fax 01770 302395. Email. arran@ayrshire-arran.com
Isle of Bute
14 Victoria Street, Rothesay , Isle of Bute. Opposite the pier. Tel. 01700 502151. Fax 01700 505156.
Isle of Cumbrae
(Seasonal) 28 Stuart Street, Millport, opposite the pier. Tel. 01475 530753.
Kilmarnock
Bank Street, just off town centre. Tel. 01563 539090. Fax 01563 572409. Email. kilmarnock@ayrshire-arran.com
Largs
The Railway Station. Tel. 01475 673765. Fax 01475 676297. Email. ayr@ayrshire-arran.com
Mauchline
National Burns Memorial Tower, Kilmarnock Road. Tel. 01290 551916.
Troon
(Seasonal) South Beach. Tel. 01292 317696.

Useful Websites
Most of these have not been mentioned previously.
This is not by any stretch of the imagination a comprehensive list, as new sites are always being launched, but it does cover most of the subjects in the book.
If you can't find what you're after in this list, type the subject into any good search engine. I like www.ask.co.uk If you don't know what I'm talking about, find someone who does!

Ayrshire
www.ayrshirehistory.org has lots of interesting articles, and many useful links.
www.ayrshireroots.com is a helpful site, links to many towns, genealogy and news.
Ayrshire & Arran Tourist Board
www.ayrshire-arran.com - Information on accommodation, shopping, etc, plus links to other sites, including business sites.
Campsites
www.mccoy-camping.co.uk/scotwestcent/listwest.htm - A comprehensive list of sites in West and South Scotland, with phone numbers and directions.

Caravanning

www.caravan-sitefinder.co.uk - A huge site with links to everything you'll ever need to know about UK sites, vans, equipment, insurance, etc, etc. See above for details of Camping and Caravanning Club.

Curling

www.curlingshoes.com is not only a retail site, but is also the home of the British Curling Association, and you will find links to all sorts of curling-related stuff.
www.brown.edu/Student/Brown_Curling_Club/info/expl.html will give you a sensible, easy-to-understand explanation of the game and how to play it.

District Councils

Details of local Council leisure services, phone numbers, addresses, that sort of thing. Go to:
www.north-ayrshire.gov.uk or www.east-ayrshire.gov.uk or www.south-ayrshire.gov.uk

Genealogy

www.ayrshirehistory.org.uk/Links/htm will link to all kinds of Ayrshire Family History sites and National archives. Have you also tried looking up the reference 'Genealogy' in the index?
www.rootsweb.com is an American site, but useful for general Scottish usage.
www.rootsweb.com/~sctayr/index.htm is another good place for Ayrshire subjects.
www.genuki/org/big/sct/ will give you a huge amount of Scottish genealogy
information and links.

Historic Scotland - www.historic-scotland.gov.uk

National Trust For Scotland - www.nts.org.uk

Paddle Steamer 'Waverley'

www.waverleyexcursions.co.uk - the official site, with the story of the ship and online booking service.
www.pswaverley.org - the unofficial site, but full of photos and information about the Waverley and other paddle steamers, and links to loads of 'steameriana', if there is such a word.

Robert Burns

www.robertburns.org - This enormous site has EVERYTHING about Burns and his works. Want a translation? Get it here. Want the Complete Burns Encyclopaedia? Get it here.
www.thing.net/~strato - This is a great site by a guy in New York who organises his own family Burns Supper. It details all you need to know, complete with sample running orders and speeches.
www.rabbie-burns.com - More details about how to organise a Burns Supper. It's more formal than the previous site, but still interesting.

Scotland in general

www.rampantscotland.com - as they say, they have over 1000 pages and over 10,000 links. Check the 'Parliamo Scots' link. I love the 'insults' section.
www.scotlandonline.com - A huge Scottish website, containing everything Scottish, ancient and modern, with links to many other interesting sites. Highly recommended.
www.electricscotland.com - More links to more Scottish stuff.
www.aboutscotland.com - ditto.

www.tartanweb.net - like a large Scottish magazine.
www.scotland.org - links to dozens of Scottish sites, for business or pleasure.
www.scotnet.de - a very good German site, but in English. Offers factual thumbnail sketches of Scottish history and the main players, with lots of stuff I haven't seen on other sites. Want to find out the history of our flag? Go here.
www.smart.net/~tak/haggis.html - this is a modest-looking but comprehensive site, by an American guy who works for NASA, I think. It's all about the humble haggis, with recipes for all flavours of haggis containing all sorts of ingredients you'd never think of. Very, very interesting.

Scotland Tourist Information
www.visitscotland.com The official Scottish Tourist Board website.
www.holiday.scotland.net Another huge site with information about touring Scotland, what to see, where to stay, etc. Highly recommended.

Scottish Youth Hostels Association
www.syha.org.uk - see below.

Youth Hostels
Firstly, Youth Hostels are not only for youths, but for families, too. Secondly, standards are high in most hostels, much higher than in my young days. Separate, secure rooms and meals are available in big city hostels, and many others offer at least a Continental breakfast. If you're really on a budget, they're worth considering, as the joining fee is only a few pounds, and the 'per night' rate is low too. Ayrshire has but one hostel at 5 Craigweil Road, Ayr, Tel. 01292 262322, but it could be used as a base for travelling around, of course.
There are two hostels on Arran, one in Lochranza, tel. 01770 830631, and one in Whiting Bay, tel. 01770 700339. All are in the towns, so it's not a long walk to the pub! Other details from Scottish Youth Hostels HQ, Tel. 01786 891400.

Index

Andy Baird was born in Ayrshire in 1952, still lives there, but is allowed out occasionally, even abroad. Happily married to Pat with a daughter Claire and two grandsons Cameron and Christopher (*'How did all that happen?'* he asks rhetorically), he has worked in professional Theatre, but mostly in the Television industry, currently as a freelance.

His varied interests include amateur theatre, gardening, movies, science fiction, history and music of many types. He enjoys travel, the company of friends, curries, good TV documentaries and comedy programmes, and wearing loud shirts, sometimes all these things at once.

His ambition is to stop smoking and lose weight - sorry, his <u>two</u> ambitions are to stop smoking and lose weight, and travel around America - sorry, he has <u>three</u> ambitions - to stop smok......oh never mind.

Thanks

I thank Nick Smalley, his wife May, and the production team at Westward Media for their enthusiasm and fast turnaround. Nick was very keen from the start, and kept me regularly informed about progress. Cheers Nick, now you can get to bed at a decent time!

I repeat my thanks to my dear wife, for her tolerance and forbearance while domestic duties of all types went undone. She complained only rarely, assisted with proof reading, laughed at my jokes, curbed my literary excesses, and indulged me as I went off on my own seeking information, or literally, chasing the deer.

Andy

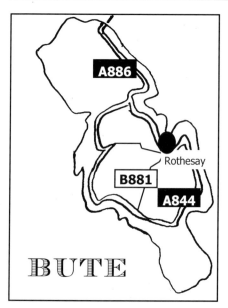

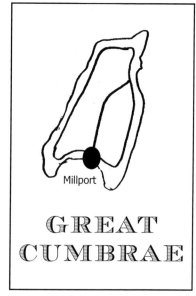

IMPORTANT: These maps are included to give an idea of **<u>approximate</u>** location only.
It is suggested that a proper map (Ordnance Survey or similar) is used for detailed route planning.

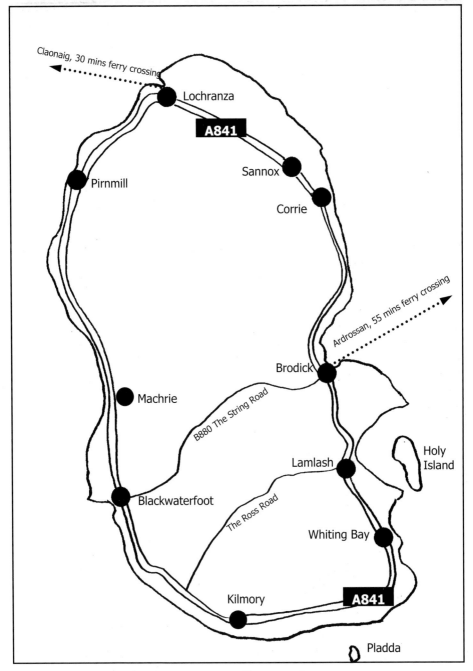

Claonaig, 30 mins ferry crossing

Lochranza

A841

Sannox

Corrie

Pirnmill

Ardrossan, 55 mins ferry crossing

Brodick

Machrie

B880 The String Road

Holy Island

Lamlash

Blackwaterfoot

The Ross Road

Whiting Bay

Kilmory

A841

Pladda

THE ISLE OF ARRAN

IMPORTANT: These maps are included to give an idea of **approximate** location only.
It is suggested that a proper map (Ordnance Survey or similar) is used for detailed route planning.

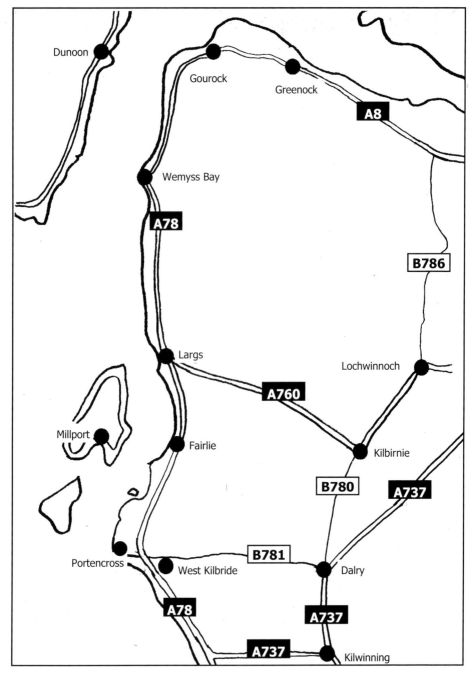

NORTH AYRSHIRE

IMPORTANT: These maps are included to give an idea of **approximate** location only.
It is suggested that a proper map (Ordnance Survey or similar) is used for detailed route planning.

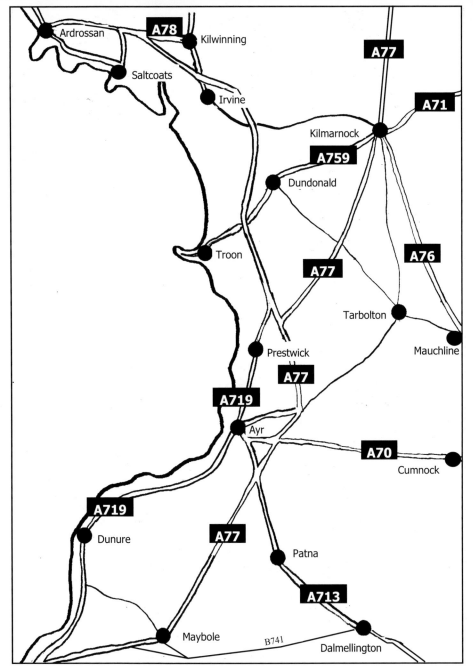

SOUTH & EAST AYRSHIRE

IMPORTANT: These maps are included to give an idea of **approximate** location only.
It is suggested that a proper map (Ordnance Survey or similar) is used for detailed route planning.

Follow The Countryside Code

- Enjoy the countryside and respect its life and work
- Guard against all risk of fire
- Fasten all gates
- Keep your dogs under close control
- Keep to public paths when crossing farmland
- Use gates or stiles to cross fences, hedges or walls
- Leave livestock, crops and machinery alone
- Take your rubbish home with you
- Protect wildlife, plants and trees
- Take special care on country roads
- Make no unnecessary noise
- Help to keep all water clean, don't tip waste of any kind into rivers or streams

We will send you a FREE copy of one of our other Scottish publications with every order for an additional copy of

"Brush Up Your Ayrshire"

see also the voucher on page 157
(the value of the gift publication is £7-95 or greater
and this offer is available only whilst stocks last).

Orders from the UK

Send a cheque or postal order for **£11-95** (which includes post & packing)
made payable to 'Westward Media' to the address shown below.

If ordering more than one copy, please deduct 5% (five per cent) for each copy ordered.

Orders from *outside* the UK

Please check the list below for the appropriate rates (which includes post & packing) and send a cheque or money order for the correct amount made payable to 'Westward Media' to the address shown below.

Country/Region	Price inc. p&p	Country/Region	Price inc. p&p
Europe	€ 26.00	Australia	$ 49.00
United States	$ 27.00	New Zealand	$ 58.00
Canada	$ 39.00	Japan	¥ 3,400.00

If ordering more than one copy, please deduct 5% (five per cent) for each copy ordered.

**Westward Media Limited (Offer),
3 Five Roads, Kilwinning, Ayrshire, Scotland KA13 7JX**

Cut out these vouchers & save money on your visits.

Post us an order for another copy of

"Brush Up Your Ayrshire"

and we will send you a **FREE** copy of one of our
other Scottish publications.
(the value of the gift publication is £7-95 or greater).
Offer available only whilst stocks last.

Orders from the UK

Send a cheque or postal order for £11-95 which includes post & packing
made payable to 'Westward Media' to:
Westward Media Limited, 3 Five Roads, Kilwinning, Ayrshire KA13 7JX

Orders from outside the UK

for postage rates, please see advert on the page opposite
Alternatively, you can phone us on +44 (0)1294 550791, write to us,
or visit our website at www.westwardmedia.com

Isle of Arran Heritage Museum

Rosaburn, Brodick, Isle of Arran
Telephone: (01770) 302185

Experience how life was lived a hundred years ago.
Regular demonstrations of Rural Crafts and Skills.

Up to <u>three</u> Under 16's admitted free
when accompanied by <u>two</u> paying adults
Valid until end of 2002
Please see entry 52B in this book for opening times and details

Brush Up Your Ayrshire—Tel: 01294 550791

157

Nothing *(noun)*: no thing, not anything, naught, nothing at all, nought, nil, not a thing, zero, zilch, without charge, gratuitously, at no cost, gratis, free.

Whichever way you say it, we can normally design, produce and print you a quality publication **ABSOLUTELY FREE.**

In-house Magazines,
Business Directories,
Guides & Brochures,
Trade Journals
Books of all kinds

For more information please contact
Westward Media Limited

3 Five Roads, Kilwinning, Ayrshire KA13 7JX

Telephone 01294 550791
E Mail info@westwardmedia.com
Website: www.westwardmedia.com

Enquiries from Tourist Attractions and Local Government establishments are particularly welcome

Cut out these vouchers & save money on your visits.

DUNASKIN OPEN AIR MUSEUM

Waterside, Patna
Telephone 01292 531144

ADMIT **TWO** FOR THE PRICE OF ONE

Dunaskin Open Air Museum tells the story of the Doon Valley and the iron works. Two audio-visual presentations,

---

ISLE OF ARRAN DISTILLERS LTD.

TWO FOR ONE VOUCHER

Please present this voucher when buying your ticket and we will give you a free ticket with our compliments

Lochranza,
Isle of Arran
Tel: 01770 830264

Fascinating guided tours
Spectacular whisky-making exhibition
Gift Shop   Distillery Restaurant   Visitor Centre

Please see entry 52F in this book for opening times and details

---

Scottish Maritime Museum

Harbourside, Irvine.
Tel: 01294 278283

ADMIT TWO FOR THE PRICE OF ONE

Please see entry 26 in this book for opening times and details